AF559572

Published by Jaico Publishing House
A-2 Jash Chambers, 7-A Sir Phirozshah Mehta Road
Fort, Mumbai - 400 001
jaicopub@jaicobooks.com
www.jaicobooks.com

THE 5 AM CLUB
MORNING MAXIMIZER JOURNAL
ISBN 978-93-90166-67-1

First Jaico Impression: 2021
Third Jaico Impression: 2024

Printed by
Thomson Press (India) Limited, New Delhi

A PERSONAL MESSAGE FROM ROBIN SHARMA

Dear Early Riser [and Human Being Dedicated to Elite Productivity + Exponential Impact],

I congratulate you for investing in this journal that I've designed to consistently upgrade your mornings, so you radically optimize your days. Our world needs more heroes and people of genuine mastery–and using this tool daily will ensure you become one of them.

Please use this journal as a companion to my #1 worldwide bestseller *The 5 AM Club*, a work that has launched a global movement of exceptional performers who rise before the dawn and apply *The 20/20/20 Formula* to materialize their primal genius.

The pages that follow will give you the opportunity to:

- record your loyalty to the morning routine I teach in the book
- review your 90 day HVTs [High Value Targets] regularly so you keep them at the front of your focus for peak execution
- stay centered on your Top 5 Values so you honor them each day, remaining true to the grandest version of yourself
- record your Daily 5 [the five micro-wins that absolutely must get done before you sleep]
- note your Nightly 3 [three things you're grateful for from the day you've just lived; this practice will help you beat the negativity bias of the human brain to concentrate on what's not working and boost deep gratitude around the current victories within your life]

- lock into a world-class Pre-Sleep Ritual [which is the key to a rare-air morning routine and maximizing The *20/20/20 Formula]*

Joining–and remaining in–*The 5 AM Club* is the one habit that lifts every other habit. It's the morning behavior that protects your creativity, multiplies your productivity and battleproofs your tranquility so you walk out into the world each day expressing the highest of your gifts, talents and bravery.

Again, bravo on investing in this journal.

Stay strong. Remain devoted. And own your mornings. So you elevate your life.

With love + respect,

Robin

P.S. I've handcrafted a powerful and content-rich learning video that will deepen your understanding of the learning models in *The 5 AM Club*, including *The Habit Installation Protocol* and *The 20/20/20 Formula*.

Access it for free at The5amClub.com/masterclass

Hope all this serves your rise beautifully. Kindest wishes.

NAME:

START DATE:

LOCATION:

IF LOST:

PHONE NUMBER

EMAIL

OWN YOUR MORNING ELEVATE YOUR LIFE

THE JOURNALING HABIT
DECONSTRUCTION

MULTIPLIES CLARITY AND AWARENESS

ACTIVATES DELIBERATE GRATITUDE

REINFORCES DAILY LEARNING

RECORDS WHERE YOU ARE WINNING

PROCESSES LOW ENERGY EMOTIONS FOR RELEASE VERSUS REPRESSION

OFFERS A PLACE TO WORK THROUGH CONFUSION

ALLOWS FOR PLANNING AND GOAL-SETTING SO EXECUTION IMPROVES

CAPTURES YOUR LIFE'S BEST EXPERIENCES

ALLOWS YOU TO RE-EXPERIENCE JOYFUL TIMES

ELEVATES YOUR CREATIVITY WHICH, WHEN TRANSLATED INTO PRODUCTIVITY, YIELDS MASTERY

Watch my free training video called "*The Journaling Deconstruction*" to see a deconstruction of my personal practice of journaling at The5amClub.com/HowToJournal

EXAMPLE PAGE

BIG 5 HIGH-VALUE TARGETS FOR THE NEXT 90 DAYS:

1. Rise at 5 am every morning to install this transformational habit.
2. Hire a personal trainer and commit to working out 3 times a week.
3. Finish the work project that will make a mark on my field.
4. Register for at least 3 events to work on my personal development.
5. Take two magnificent vacations to fuel my creativity and renew my positivity.

TOP 5 VALUES TO OPERATE BY FOR THE NEXT 90 DAYS:

1. Live daily with honesty, integrity and bravery.
2. Put peak health, a joyful family life and self-mastery first.
3. Be the kind of person who keeps their commitments.
4. Seek beauty and simple magic every day.
5. Operate in a way that expresses my heroism, fearlessness and decency.

EXAMPLE PAGE

— THE 20/20/20 FORMULA™ —

POCKET #1

5:00 AM – 5:20 AM
MOVE

COMPLETED: YES ☑ NO ☐

COMMITMENT FOR TOMORROW MORNING:
Commit to 25 push-ups

POCKET #2

5:20 AM – 5:40 AM
REFLECT

COMPLETED: YES ☑ NO ☐

COMMITMENT FOR TOMORROW MORNING:
Write in my journal for one hour about the human being and exceptionalist I wish to become

POCKET #3

5:40 AM – 6:00 AM
GROW

COMPLETED: YES ☑ NO ☐

COMMITMENT FOR TOMORROW MORNING:
Listen to The Mastery Sessions for 20 minutes

MORNING PRACTICE

5 MICRO GOALS FOR TODAY:

1. Mentor my team at 10 am
2. Go to a spin class at lunch
3. Block an hour for creative thinking
4. Have a beautiful family meal
5. Read for an hour before sleep

EVENING PRACTICE

3 TINY WINS OF THIS DAY:

1. Successfully did all I'd planned to do
2. Stayed focused versus distracted all day
3. Optimized my morning routine to win

PRE-SLEEP RITUAL DONE: YES ☑ NO ☐

MY DAILY REFLECTION

I express gratefulness for the gift of this day. I am increasing my success, growing as a person, enriching my family life and producing work that makes a deep difference to others.

Today, I commit to amplifying my productivity as well as being a force of positivity, excellence and goodness in the world. I will make the hours ahead count, living fully and completely.

I'll also spend a little more time than yesterday on my learning and growth, given that all outer triumph is a reflection of inner mastery. And I will be bold, decisive and strong.

I will see the best in others, being patient and kind as well as standing for my unique greatness as I experience the adventure of this day.

BIG 5 HIGH-VALUE TARGETS
FOR THE NEXT 90 DAYS:

1.
2.
3.
4.
5.

TOP 5 VALUES TO OPERATE BY
FOR THE NEXT 90 DAYS:

1.
2.
3.
4.
5.

DAY 01/90

— THE 20/20/20 FORMULA™ —

POCKET #1

5:00 AM
5:20 AM
MOVE

COMPLETED: YES ☐ NO ☐

COMMITMENT FOR TOMORROW MORNING:

POCKET #2

5:20 AM
5:40 AM
REFLECT

COMPLETED: YES ☐ NO ☐

COMMITMENT FOR TOMORROW MORNING:

POCKET #3

5:40 AM
6:00 AM
GROW

COMPLETED: YES ☐ NO ☐

COMMITMENT FOR TOMORROW MORNING:

MORNING PRACTICE

5 MICRO GOALS FOR TODAY:

1.
2.
3.
4.
5.

EVENING PRACTICE

3 TINY WINS OF THIS DAY:

1.
2.
3.

PRE-SLEEP RITUAL DONE: YES ☐ NO ☐

"Can't is the addiction of average."

-ROBIN SHARMA-

MY DAILY REFLECTION

DAY 02/90

— THE 20/20/20 FORMULA™ —

POCKET #1

5:00 AM
5:20 AM
MOVE

COMPLETED: YES ☐ NO ☐

COMMITMENT FOR TOMORROW MORNING:

POCKET #2

5:20 AM
5:40 AM
REFLECT

COMPLETED: YES ☐ NO ☐

COMMITMENT FOR TOMORROW MORNING:

POCKET #3

5:40 AM
6:00 AM
GROW

COMPLETED: YES ☐ NO ☐

COMMITMENT FOR TOMORROW MORNING:

MORNING PRACTICE

5 MICRO GOALS FOR TODAY:

1.
2.
3.
4.
5.

EVENING PRACTICE

3 TINY WINS OF THIS DAY:

1.
2.
3.

PRE-SLEEP RITUAL DONE: YES ☐ NO ☐

"Genius is not the realm of genetics. Genius is the realm of practice."

-ROBIN SHARMA-

MY DAILY REFLECTION

DAY 03/90

— THE 20/20/20 FORMULA™ —

POCKET #1

5:00 AM
5:20 AM
MOVE

COMPLETED: YES ☐ NO ☐

COMMITMENT FOR TOMORROW MORNING:

POCKET #2

5:20 AM
5:40 AM
REFLECT

COMPLETED: YES ☐ NO ☐

COMMITMENT FOR TOMORROW MORNING:

POCKET #3

5:40 AM
6:00 AM
GROW

COMPLETED: YES ☐ NO ☐

COMMITMENT FOR TOMORROW MORNING:

MORNING PRACTICE

5 MICRO GOALS FOR TODAY:

1.
2.
3.
4.
5.

EVENING PRACTICE

3 TINY WINS OF THIS DAY:

1.
2.
3.

PRE-SLEEP RITUAL DONE: YES ☐ NO ☐

"To have the results that only 5% of the population has, you must be willing to do what 95% of the population is unwilling to do."

-ROBIN SHARMA-

MY DAILY REFLECTION

DAY 04/90

— THE 20/20/20 FORMULA™ —

POCKET #1

5:00 AM
5:20 AM
MOVE

COMPLETED: YES ☐ NO ☐

COMMITMENT FOR TOMORROW MORNING:

POCKET #2

5:20 AM
5:40 AM
REFLECT

COMPLETED: YES ☐ NO ☐

COMMITMENT FOR TOMORROW MORNING:

POCKET #3

5:40 AM
6:00 AM
GROW

COMPLETED: YES ☐ NO ☐

COMMITMENT FOR TOMORROW MORNING:

MORNING PRACTICE

5 MICRO GOALS FOR TODAY:

1.
2.
3.
4.
5.

EVENING PRACTICE

3 TINY WINS OF THIS DAY:

1.
2.
3.

PRE-SLEEP RITUAL DONE: YES ☐ NO ☐

"Dream big. Start small. Act now."

-ROBIN SHARMA-

MY DAILY REFLECTION

DAY 05/90

— THE 20/20/20 FORMULA™ —

POCKET #1

5:00 AM
5:20 AM
MOVE

COMPLETED: YES ☐ NO ☐

COMMITMENT FOR TOMORROW MORNING:

POCKET #2

5:20 AM
5:40 AM
REFLECT

COMPLETED: YES ☐ NO ☐

COMMITMENT FOR TOMORROW MORNING:

POCKET #3

5:40 AM
6:00 AM
GROW

COMPLETED: YES ☐ NO ☐

COMMITMENT FOR TOMORROW MORNING:

MORNING PRACTICE

5 MICRO GOALS FOR TODAY:

1.
2.
3.
4.
5.

EVENING PRACTICE

3 TINY WINS OF THIS DAY:

1.
2.
3.

PRE-SLEEP RITUAL DONE: YES ☐ NO ☐

"Rather than fearing the pain of failure, worry about the arrogance of success."

-ROBIN SHARMA-

MY DAILY REFLECTION

DAY 06/90

— THE 20/20/20 FORMULA™ —

POCKET #1

5:00 AM
5:20 AM
MOVE

COMPLETED: YES ☐ NO ☐

COMMITMENT FOR TOMORROW MORNING:

POCKET #2

5:20 AM
5:40 AM
REFLECT

COMPLETED: YES ☐ NO ☐

COMMITMENT FOR TOMORROW MORNING:

POCKET #3

5:40 AM
6:00 AM
GROW

COMPLETED: YES ☐ NO ☐

COMMITMENT FOR TOMORROW MORNING:

MORNING PRACTICE

5 MICRO GOALS FOR TODAY:

1.
2.
3.
4.
5.

EVENING PRACTICE

3 TINY WINS OF THIS DAY:

1.
2.
3.

PRE-SLEEP RITUAL DONE: YES ☐ NO ☐

"The discomfort of change is better than the heartbreak of complacency."
- ROBIN SHARMA -

MY DAILY REFLECTION

DAY 07/90

— THE 20/20/20 FORMULA™ —

POCKET #1

5:00 AM
–
5:20 AM
MOVE

COMPLETED: YES ☐ NO ☐

COMMITMENT FOR TOMORROW MORNING:

POCKET #2

5:20 AM
–
5:40 AM
REFLECT

COMPLETED: YES ☐ NO ☐

COMMITMENT FOR TOMORROW MORNING:

POCKET #3

5:40 AM
–
6:00 AM
GROW

COMPLETED: YES ☐ NO ☐

COMMITMENT FOR TOMORROW MORNING:

MORNING PRACTICE

5 MICRO GOALS FOR TODAY:

1.
2.
3.
4.
5.

EVENING PRACTICE

3 TINY WINS OF THIS DAY:

1.
2.
3.

PRE-SLEEP RITUAL DONE: YES ☐ NO ☐

"Elite production without quiet vacation causes lasting depletion."
-ROBIN SHARMA-

MY DAILY REFLECTION

STRATEGIC WEEKLY REVIEW

WHAT WORKED WELL THIS WEEK?

WHAT NEEDS TO BE IMPROVED?

WHAT CAN I CELEBRATE MYSELF FOR?

To download *The Weekly Planning Blueprint [WPB]* that I use to build out my own weeks, go to: The5amClub.com/weeklyplanner

MY 3 MAIN PERSONAL GOALS FOR THE WEEK AHEAD:

1.
2.
3.

MY 3 MAIN WORK GOALS FOR THE WEEK AHEAD:

1.
2.
3.

GENERAL OPTIMIZATIONS FOR THE WEEK AHEAD:

1.
2.
3.

DAY 08/90

— THE 20/20/20 FORMULA™ —

POCKET #1

5:00 AM
5:20 AM
MOVE

COMPLETED: YES ☐ NO ☐

COMMITMENT FOR TOMORROW MORNING:

POCKET #2

5:20 AM
5:40 AM
REFLECT

COMPLETED: YES ☐ NO ☐

COMMITMENT FOR TOMORROW MORNING:

POCKET #3

5:40 AM
6:00 AM
GROW

COMPLETED: YES ☐ NO ☐

COMMITMENT FOR TOMORROW MORNING:

MORNING PRACTICE

5 MICRO GOALS FOR TODAY:

1.
2.
3.
4.
5.

EVENING PRACTICE

3 TINY WINS OF THIS DAY:

1.
2.
3.

PRE-SLEEP RITUAL DONE: YES ☐ NO ☐

"Leadership is about making a difference, right where you're planted."

- ROBIN SHARMA -

MY DAILY REFLECTION

DAY 09/90

— THE 20/20/20 FORMULA™ —

POCKET #1

5:00 AM
—
5:20 AM
MOVE

COMPLETED: YES ☐ NO ☐

COMMITMENT FOR TOMORROW MORNING:

POCKET #2

5:20 AM
—
5:40 AM
REFLECT

COMPLETED: YES ☐ NO ☐

COMMITMENT FOR TOMORROW MORNING:

POCKET #3

5:40 AM
—
6:00 AM
GROW

COMPLETED: YES ☐ NO ☐

COMMITMENT FOR TOMORROW MORNING:

MORNING PRACTICE

5 MICRO GOALS FOR TODAY:

1.
2.
3.
4.
5.

EVENING PRACTICE

3 TINY WINS OF THIS DAY:

1.
2.
3.

PRE-SLEEP RITUAL DONE: YES ☐ NO ☐

"You can be creative. Or you can be distracted. But you can't be both."

-ROBIN SHARMA-

MY DAILY REFLECTION

DAY 10/90

— THE 20/20/20 FORMULA™ —

POCKET #1

5:00 AM
–
5:20 AM
MOVE

COMPLETED: YES ☐ NO ☐

COMMITMENT FOR TOMORROW MORNING:

POCKET #2

5:20 AM
–
5:40 AM
REFLECT

COMPLETED: YES ☐ NO ☐

COMMITMENT FOR TOMORROW MORNING:

POCKET #3

5:40 AM
–
6:00 AM
GROW

COMPLETED: YES ☐ NO ☐

COMMITMENT FOR TOMORROW MORNING:

MORNING PRACTICE

5 MICRO GOALS FOR TODAY:

1.
2.
3.
4.
5.

EVENING PRACTICE

3 TINY WINS OF THIS DAY:

1.
2.
3.

PRE-SLEEP RITUAL DONE: YES ☐ NO ☐

"A problem is only a problem if you choose to see it as a problem."

-ROBIN SHARMA-

MY DAILY REFLECTION

DAY 11/90

— THE 20/20/20 FORMULA™ —

POCKET #1

5:00 AM
—
5:20 AM
MOVE

COMPLETED: YES ☐ NO ☐

COMMITMENT FOR TOMORROW MORNING:

POCKET #2

5:20 AM
—
5:40 AM
REFLECT

COMPLETED: YES ☐ NO ☐

COMMITMENT FOR TOMORROW MORNING:

POCKET #3

5:40 AM
—
6:00 AM
GROW

COMPLETED: YES ☐ NO ☐

COMMITMENT FOR TOMORROW MORNING:

MORNING PRACTICE

5 MICRO GOALS FOR TODAY:

1.
2.
3.
4.
5.

EVENING PRACTICE

3 TINY WINS OF THIS DAY:

1.
2.
3.

PRE-SLEEP RITUAL DONE: YES ☐ NO ☐

"Start being an imaginationalist—one of those rare individuals who leads from the nobility of your future versus via the prison bars of your past."

-ROBIN SHARMA-

MY DAILY REFLECTION

DAY 12/90

— THE 20/20/20 FORMULA™ —

POCKET #1

5:00 AM
–
5:20 AM
MOVE

COMPLETED: YES ☐ NO ☐

COMMITMENT FOR TOMORROW MORNING:

POCKET #2

5:20 AM
–
5:40 AM
REFLECT

COMPLETED: YES ☐ NO ☐

COMMITMENT FOR TOMORROW MORNING:

POCKET #3

5:40 AM
–
6:00 AM
GROW

COMPLETED: YES ☐ NO ☐

COMMITMENT FOR TOMORROW MORNING:

MORNING PRACTICE

5 MICRO GOALS FOR TODAY:

1.
2.
3.
4.
5.

EVENING PRACTICE

3 TINY WINS OF THIS DAY:

1.
2.
3.

PRE-SLEEP RITUAL DONE: YES ☐ NO ☐

"Limitation is nothing more than a mentality that too many good people practice daily until they believe it's a reality."

-ROBIN SHARMA-

MY DAILY REFLECTION

DAY 13/90

— THE 20/20/20 FORMULA™ —

POCKET #1

5:00 AM
–
5:20 AM
MOVE

COMPLETED: YES ☐ NO ☐

COMMITMENT FOR TOMORROW MORNING:

POCKET #2

5:20 AM
–
5:40 AM
REFLECT

COMPLETED: YES ☐ NO ☐

COMMITMENT FOR TOMORROW MORNING:

POCKET #3

5:40 AM
–
6:00 AM
GROW

COMPLETED: YES ☐ NO ☐

COMMITMENT FOR TOMORROW MORNING:

MORNING PRACTICE

5 MICRO GOALS FOR TODAY:

1.
2.
3.
4.
5.

EVENING PRACTICE

3 TINY WINS OF THIS DAY:

1.
2.
3.

PRE-SLEEP RITUAL DONE: YES ☐ NO ☐

"Being yourself is a love letter to the world."

-ROBIN SHARMA-

MY DAILY REFLECTION

DAY 14/90

— THE 20/20/20 FORMULA™ —

POCKET #1

5:00 AM
–
5:20 AM
MOVE

COMPLETED: YES ☐ NO ☐

COMMITMENT FOR TOMORROW MORNING:

POCKET #2

5:20 AM
–
5:40 AM
REFLECT

COMPLETED: YES ☐ NO ☐

COMMITMENT FOR TOMORROW MORNING:

POCKET #3

5:40 AM
–
6:00 AM
GROW

COMPLETED: YES ☐ NO ☐

COMMITMENT FOR TOMORROW MORNING:

MORNING PRACTICE

5 MICRO GOALS FOR TODAY:

1.
2.
3.
4.
5.

EVENING PRACTICE

3 TINY WINS OF THIS DAY:

1.
2.
3.

PRE-SLEEP RITUAL DONE: YES ☐ NO ☐

"Greatness comes by beginning something that doesn't end with you."

-ROBIN SHARMA-

MY DAILY REFLECTION

STRATEGIC WEEKLY REVIEW

WHAT WORKED WELL THIS WEEK?

WHAT NEEDS TO BE IMPROVED?

WHAT CAN I CELEBRATE MYSELF FOR?

To download *The Weekly Planning Blueprint [WPB]* that I use to build out my own weeks, go to: The5amClub.com/weeklyplanner

MY 3 MAIN PERSONAL GOALS FOR THE WEEK AHEAD:

1.

2.

3.

MY 3 MAIN WORK GOALS FOR THE WEEK AHEAD:

1.

2.

3.

GENERAL OPTIMIZATIONS FOR THE WEEK AHEAD:

1.

2.

3.

DAY 15/90

— THE 20/20/20 FORMULA™ —

POCKET #1

5:00 AM – 5:20 AM
MOVE

COMPLETED: YES ☐ NO ☐

COMMITMENT FOR TOMORROW MORNING:

POCKET #2

5:20 AM – 5:40 AM
REFLECT

COMPLETED: YES ☐ NO ☐

COMMITMENT FOR TOMORROW MORNING:

POCKET #3

5:40 AM – 6:00 AM
GROW

COMPLETED: YES ☐ NO ☐

COMMITMENT FOR TOMORROW MORNING:

MORNING PRACTICE

5 MICRO GOALS FOR TODAY:

1.
2.
3.
4.
5.

EVENING PRACTICE

3 TINY WINS OF THIS DAY:

1.
2.
3.

PRE-SLEEP RITUAL DONE: YES ☐ NO ☐

"The soreness of growth is so much less expensive than the devastating cost of regret."

-ROBIN SHARMA-

MY DAILY REFLECTION

DAY 16/90

— THE 20/20/20 FORMULA™ —

POCKET #1

5:00 AM
5:20 AM
MOVE

COMPLETED: YES ☐ NO ☐

COMMITMENT FOR TOMORROW MORNING:

POCKET #2

5:20 AM
5:40 AM
REFLECT

COMPLETED: YES ☐ NO ☐

COMMITMENT FOR TOMORROW MORNING:

POCKET #3

5:40 AM
6:00 AM
GROW

COMPLETED: YES ☐ NO ☐

COMMITMENT FOR TOMORROW MORNING:

MORNING PRACTICE

5 MICRO GOALS FOR TODAY:

1.
2.
3.
4.
5.

EVENING PRACTICE

3 TINY WINS OF THIS DAY:

1.
2.
3.

PRE-SLEEP RITUAL DONE: YES ☐ NO ☐

"Your 'I Can' is more important than your IQ."
-ROBIN SHARMA-

MY DAILY REFLECTION

DAY 17/90

— THE 20/20/20 FORMULA™ —

POCKET #1

5:00 AM
5:20 AM
MOVE

COMPLETED: YES ☐ NO ☐

COMMITMENT FOR TOMORROW MORNING:

POCKET #2

5:20 AM
5:40 AM
REFLECT

COMPLETED: YES ☐ NO ☐

COMMITMENT FOR TOMORROW MORNING:

POCKET #3

5:40 AM
6:00 AM
GROW

COMPLETED: YES ☐ NO ☐

COMMITMENT FOR TOMORROW MORNING:

MORNING PRACTICE

5 MICRO GOALS FOR TODAY:

1.
2.
3.
4.
5.

EVENING PRACTICE

3 TINY WINS OF THIS DAY:

1.
2.
3.

PRE-SLEEP RITUAL DONE: YES ☐ NO ☐

"Those who can, do. Those who can't, criticize."

-ROBIN SHARMA-

MY DAILY REFLECTION

DAY 18/90

— THE 20/20/20 FORMULA™ —

POCKET #1

5:00 AM – 5:20 AM
MOVE

COMPLETED: YES ☐ NO ☐

COMMITMENT FOR TOMORROW MORNING:

POCKET #2

5:20 AM – 5:40 AM
REFLECT

COMPLETED: YES ☐ NO ☐

COMMITMENT FOR TOMORROW MORNING:

POCKET #3

5:40 AM – 6:00 AM
GROW

COMPLETED: YES ☐ NO ☐

COMMITMENT FOR TOMORROW MORNING:

MORNING PRACTICE

5 MICRO GOALS FOR TODAY:

1.
2.
3.
4.
5.

EVENING PRACTICE

3 TINY WINS OF THIS DAY:

1.
2.
3.

PRE-SLEEP RITUAL DONE: YES ☐ NO ☐

"Stop managing your time. Start managing your focus."

-ROBIN SHARMA-

MY DAILY REFLECTION

DAY 19/90

— THE 20/20/20 FORMULA™ —

POCKET #1

5:00 AM – 5:20 AM
MOVE

COMPLETED: YES ☐ NO ☐

COMMITMENT FOR TOMORROW MORNING:

POCKET #2

5:20 AM – 5:40 AM
REFLECT

COMPLETED: YES ☐ NO ☐

COMMITMENT FOR TOMORROW MORNING:

POCKET #3

5:40 AM – 6:00 AM
GROW

COMPLETED: YES ☐ NO ☐

COMMITMENT FOR TOMORROW MORNING:

MORNING PRACTICE

5 MICRO GOALS FOR TODAY:

1.
2.
3.
4.
5.

EVENING PRACTICE

3 TINY WINS OF THIS DAY:

1.
2.
3.

PRE-SLEEP RITUAL DONE: YES ☐ NO ☐

"It doesn't matter if people understand your intentions so long as you understand your intentions."

- ROBIN SHARMA -

MY DAILY REFLECTION

DAY 20/90

— THE 20/20/20 FORMULA™ —

POCKET #1

5:00 AM
–
5:20 AM
MOVE

COMPLETED: YES ☐ NO ☐

COMMITMENT FOR TOMORROW MORNING:

____

____

POCKET #2

5:20 AM
–
5:40 AM
REFLECT

COMPLETED: YES ☐ NO ☐

COMMITMENT FOR TOMORROW MORNING:

____

____

POCKET #3

5:40 AM
–
6:00 AM
GROW

COMPLETED: YES ☐ NO ☐

COMMITMENT FOR TOMORROW MORNING:

____

____

MORNING PRACTICE

5 MICRO GOALS FOR TODAY:

1. ______________________________
2. ______________________________
3. ______________________________
4. ______________________________
5. ______________________________

EVENING PRACTICE

3 TINY WINS OF THIS DAY:

1. ______________________________
2. ______________________________
3. ______________________________

PRE-SLEEP RITUAL DONE: YES ☐ NO ☐

"Mind management is the essence of life management."
-ROBIN SHARMA-

MY DAILY REFLECTION

DAY 21/90

— THE 20/20/20 FORMULA™ —

POCKET #1

5:00 AM
5:20 AM
MOVE

COMPLETED: YES ☐ NO ☐

COMMITMENT FOR TOMORROW MORNING:

POCKET #2

5:20 AM
5:40 AM
REFLECT

COMPLETED: YES ☐ NO ☐

COMMITMENT FOR TOMORROW MORNING:

POCKET #3

5:40 AM
6:00 AM
GROW

COMPLETED: YES ☐ NO ☐

COMMITMENT FOR TOMORROW MORNING:

MORNING PRACTICE

5 MICRO GOALS FOR TODAY:

1.
2.
3.
4.
5.

EVENING PRACTICE

3 TINY WINS OF THIS DAY:

1.
2.
3.

PRE-SLEEP RITUAL DONE: YES ☐ NO ☐

"Beneath mastery lives consistency. Surrounding excellence lies persistence."

-ROBIN SHARMA-

MY DAILY REFLECTION

STRATEGIC WEEKLY REVIEW

WHAT WORKED WELL THIS WEEK?

WHAT NEEDS TO BE IMPROVED?

WHAT CAN I CELEBRATE MYSELF FOR?

To download *The Weekly Planning Blueprint [WPB]* that I use to build out my own weeks, go to: The5amClub.com/weeklyplanner

MY 3 MAIN PERSONAL GOALS FOR THE WEEK AHEAD:

1.
2.
3.

MY 3 MAIN WORK GOALS FOR THE WEEK AHEAD:

1.
2.
3.

GENERAL OPTIMIZATIONS FOR THE WEEK AHEAD:

1.
2.
3.

DAY 22/90

— THE 20/20/20 FORMULA™ —

POCKET #1

5:00 AM
–
5:20 AM
MOVE

COMPLETED: YES ☐ NO ☐

COMMITMENT FOR TOMORROW MORNING:

POCKET #2

5:20 AM
–
5:40 AM
REFLECT

COMPLETED: YES ☐ NO ☐

COMMITMENT FOR TOMORROW MORNING:

POCKET #3

5:40 AM
–
6:00 AM
GROW

COMPLETED: YES ☐ NO ☐

COMMITMENT FOR TOMORROW MORNING:

MORNING PRACTICE

5 MICRO GOALS FOR TODAY:

1.
2.
3.
4.
5.

EVENING PRACTICE

3 TINY WINS OF THIS DAY:

1.
2.
3.

PRE-SLEEP RITUAL DONE: YES ☐ NO ☐

"Huge achievement is less about your genetics and more about your rituals."

-ROBIN SHARMA-

MY DAILY REFLECTION

DAY 23/90

— THE 20/20/20 FORMULA™ —

POCKET #1

5:00 AM
5:20 AM
MOVE

COMPLETED: YES ☐ NO ☐

COMMITMENT FOR TOMORROW MORNING:

POCKET #2

5:20 AM
5:40 AM
REFLECT

COMPLETED: YES ☐ NO ☐

COMMITMENT FOR TOMORROW MORNING:

POCKET #3

5:40 AM
6:00 AM
GROW

COMPLETED: YES ☐ NO ☐

COMMITMENT FOR TOMORROW MORNING:

MORNING PRACTICE

5 MICRO GOALS FOR TODAY:

1.
2.
3.
4.
5.

EVENING PRACTICE

3 TINY WINS OF THIS DAY:

1.
2.
3.

PRE-SLEEP RITUAL DONE: YES ☐ NO ☐

"It's smarter to focus on quality versus speed."
-ROBIN SHARMA-

MY DAILY REFLECTION

DAY 24/90

— THE 20/20/20 FORMULA™ —

POCKET #1

5:00 AM
—
5:20 AM
MOVE

COMPLETED: YES ☐ NO ☐

COMMITMENT FOR TOMORROW MORNING:

POCKET #2

5:20 AM
—
5:40 AM
REFLECT

COMPLETED: YES ☐ NO ☐

COMMITMENT FOR TOMORROW MORNING:

POCKET #3

5:40 AM
—
6:00 AM
GROW

COMPLETED: YES ☐ NO ☐

COMMITMENT FOR TOMORROW MORNING:

MORNING PRACTICE

5 MICRO GOALS FOR TODAY:

1.
2.
3.
4.
5.

EVENING PRACTICE

3 TINY WINS OF THIS DAY:

1.
2.
3.

PRE-SLEEP RITUAL DONE: YES ☐ NO ☐

"You become your conversations. You'll think like your associations. And your life will look a lot like the lives of the people you spend most of your time with."

- ROBIN SHARMA -

MY DAILY REFLECTION

DAY 25/90

— THE 20/20/20 FORMULA™ —

POCKET #1

5:00 AM
5:20 AM
MOVE

COMPLETED: YES ☐ NO ☐

COMMITMENT FOR TOMORROW MORNING:

POCKET #2

5:20 AM
5:40 AM
REFLECT

COMPLETED: YES ☐ NO ☐

COMMITMENT FOR TOMORROW MORNING:

POCKET #3

5:40 AM
6:00 AM
GROW

COMPLETED: YES ☐ NO ☐

COMMITMENT FOR TOMORROW MORNING:

MORNING PRACTICE

5 MICRO GOALS FOR TODAY:

1.
2.
3.
4.
5.

EVENING PRACTICE

3 TINY WINS OF THIS DAY:

1.
2.
3.

PRE-SLEEP RITUAL DONE: YES ☐ NO ☐

"Just remember, you can't win the game if you don't even play it."

-ROBIN SHARMA-

MY DAILY REFLECTION

DAY 26/90

— THE 20/20/20 FORMULA™ —

POCKET #1

5:00 AM
5:20 AM
MOVE

COMPLETED: YES ☐ NO ☐

COMMITMENT FOR TOMORROW MORNING:

POCKET #2

5:20 AM
5:40 AM
REFLECT

COMPLETED: YES ☐ NO ☐

COMMITMENT FOR TOMORROW MORNING:

POCKET #3

5:40 AM
6:00 AM
GROW

COMPLETED: YES ☐ NO ☐

COMMITMENT FOR TOMORROW MORNING:

MORNING PRACTICE

5 MICRO GOALS FOR TODAY:

1.
2.
3.
4.
5.

EVENING PRACTICE

3 TINY WINS OF THIS DAY:

1.
2.
3.

PRE-SLEEP RITUAL DONE: YES ☐ NO ☐

"Success without honor is nothing. Victory without decency is a waste."
-ROBIN SHARMA-

MY DAILY REFLECTION

DAY 27/90

— THE 20/20/20 FORMULA™ —

POCKET #1

5:00 AM
5:20 AM
MOVE

COMPLETED: YES ☐ NO ☐

COMMITMENT FOR TOMORROW MORNING:

POCKET #2

5:20 AM
5:40 AM
REFLECT

COMPLETED: YES ☐ NO ☐

COMMITMENT FOR TOMORROW MORNING:

POCKET #3

5:40 AM
6:00 AM
GROW

COMPLETED: YES ☐ NO ☐

COMMITMENT FOR TOMORROW MORNING:

MORNING PRACTICE

5 MICRO GOALS FOR TODAY:

1.
2.
3.
4.
5.

EVENING PRACTICE

3 TINY WINS OF THIS DAY:

1.
2.
3.

PRE-SLEEP RITUAL DONE: YES ☐ NO ☐

"Your life is your autobiography. Write an epic."

-ROBIN SHARMA-

MY DAILY REFLECTION

DAY 28/90

— THE 20/20/20 FORMULA™ —

POCKET #1

5:00 AM
–
5:20 AM
MOVE

COMPLETED: YES ☐ NO ☐

COMMITMENT FOR TOMORROW MORNING:

____

____

POCKET #2

5:20 AM
–
5:40 AM
REFLECT

COMPLETED: YES ☐ NO ☐

COMMITMENT FOR TOMORROW MORNING:

____

____

POCKET #3

5:40 AM
–
6:00 AM
GROW

COMPLETED: YES ☐ NO ☐

COMMITMENT FOR TOMORROW MORNING:

____

____

MORNING PRACTICE

5 MICRO GOALS FOR TODAY:

1. ______________________________
2. ______________________________
3. ______________________________
4. ______________________________
5. ______________________________

EVENING PRACTICE

3 TINY WINS OF THIS DAY:

1. ______________________________
2. ______________________________
3. ______________________________

PRE-SLEEP RITUAL DONE: YES ☐ NO ☐

"The more you go to the edge of your limits, the more your limits will expand."

-ROBIN SHARMA-

MY DAILY REFLECTION

STRATEGIC WEEKLY REVIEW

WHAT WORKED WELL THIS WEEK?

WHAT NEEDS TO BE IMPROVED?

WHAT CAN I CELEBRATE MYSELF FOR?

To download *The Weekly Planning Blueprint [WPB]* that I use to build out my own weeks, go to: The5amClub.com/weeklyplanner

MY 3 MAIN PERSONAL GOALS FOR THE WEEK AHEAD:

1.
2.
3.

MY 3 MAIN WORK GOALS FOR THE WEEK AHEAD:

1.
2.
3.

GENERAL OPTIMIZATIONS FOR THE WEEK AHEAD:

1.
2.
3.

DAY 29/90

— THE 20/20/20 FORMULA™ —

POCKET #1

5:00 AM
–
5:20 AM
MOVE

COMPLETED: YES ☐ NO ☐

COMMITMENT FOR TOMORROW MORNING:

POCKET #2

5:20 AM
–
5:40 AM
REFLECT

COMPLETED: YES ☐ NO ☐

COMMITMENT FOR TOMORROW MORNING:

POCKET #3

5:40 AM
–
6:00 AM
GROW

COMPLETED: YES ☐ NO ☐

COMMITMENT FOR TOMORROW MORNING:

MORNING PRACTICE

5 MICRO GOALS FOR TODAY:

1.
2.
3.
4.
5.

EVENING PRACTICE

3 TINY WINS OF THIS DAY:

1.
2.
3.

PRE-SLEEP RITUAL DONE: YES ☐ NO ☐

"Copyists never change the world. Originalists do."
- ROBIN SHARMA -

MY DAILY REFLECTION

DAY 30/90

— THE 20/20/20 FORMULA™ —

POCKET #1

5:00 AM
5:20 AM
MOVE

COMPLETED: YES ☐ NO ☐

COMMITMENT FOR TOMORROW MORNING:

POCKET #2

5:20 AM
5:40 AM
REFLECT

COMPLETED: YES ☐ NO ☐

COMMITMENT FOR TOMORROW MORNING:

POCKET #3

5:40 AM
6:00 AM
GROW

COMPLETED: YES ☐ NO ☐

COMMITMENT FOR TOMORROW MORNING:

MORNING PRACTICE

5 MICRO GOALS FOR TODAY:

1.
2.
3.
4.
5.

EVENING PRACTICE

3 TINY WINS OF THIS DAY:

1.
2.
3.

PRE-SLEEP RITUAL DONE: YES ☐ NO ☐

"It doesn't matter where you start. Only that you begin."

-ROBIN SHARMA-

MY DAILY REFLECTION

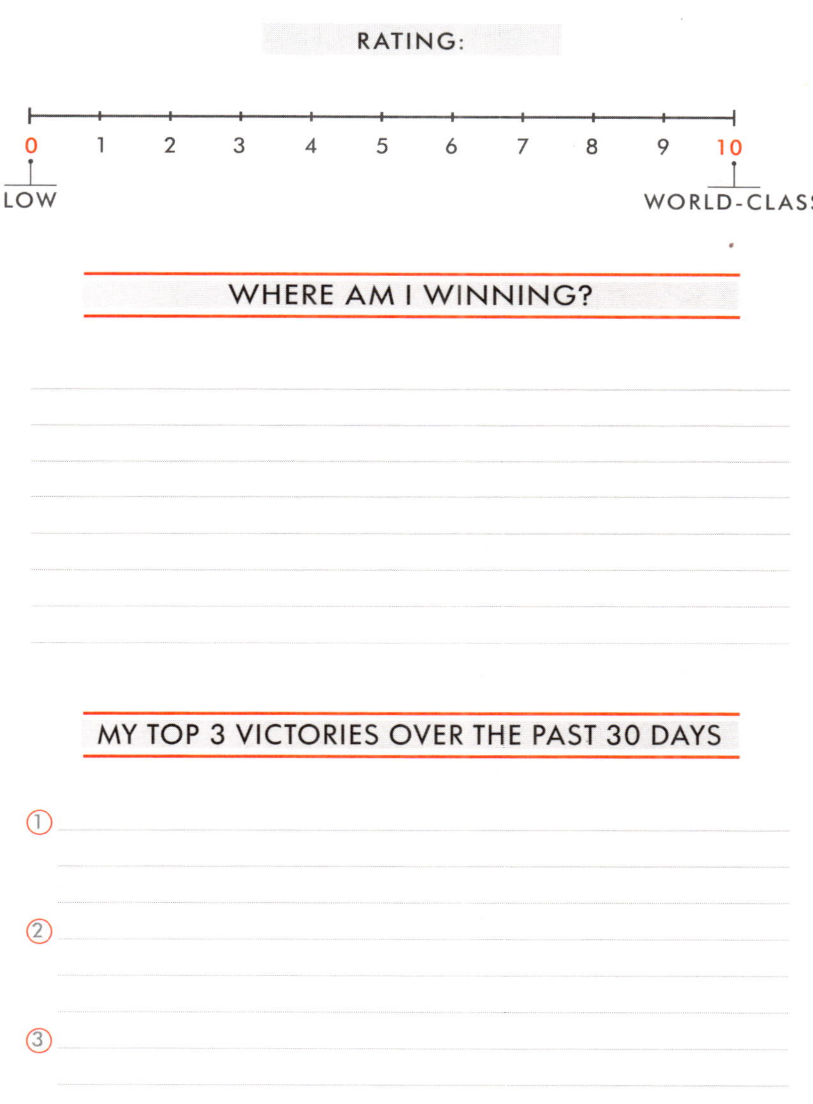

30 DAY PERFORMANCE INQUIRY

RATING:

0 1 2 3 4 5 6 7 8 9 10

LOW — WORLD-CLASS

WHERE AM I WINNING?

MY TOP 3 VICTORIES OVER THE PAST 30 DAYS

1.

2.

3.

MY IDEAL NEXT 30 DAYS AS A DRAWING

5 PROGRESS ACCELERATORS THAT WILL MAKE THE NEXT 30 DAYS MY BEST 30 DAYS YET

1.

2.

3.

4.

5.

DAY 31/90

— THE 20/20/20 FORMULA™ —

POCKET #1

5:00 AM
–
5:20 AM
MOVE

COMPLETED: YES ☐ NO ☐

COMMITMENT FOR TOMORROW MORNING:

POCKET #2

5:20 AM
–
5:40 AM
REFLECT

COMPLETED: YES ☐ NO ☐

COMMITMENT FOR TOMORROW MORNING:

POCKET #3

5:40 AM
–
6:00 AM
GROW

COMPLETED: YES ☐ NO ☐

COMMITMENT FOR TOMORROW MORNING:

MORNING PRACTICE

5 MICRO GOALS FOR TODAY:

1.
2.
3.
4.
5.

EVENING PRACTICE

3 TINY WINS OF THIS DAY:

1.
2.
3.

PRE-SLEEP RITUAL DONE: YES ☐ NO ☐

"Greatness on the outside begins within."

-ROBIN SHARMA-

MY DAILY REFLECTION

DAY 32/90

— THE 20/20/20 FORMULA™ —

POCKET #1

5:00 AM
5:20 AM
MOVE

COMPLETED: YES ☐ NO ☐

COMMITMENT FOR TOMORROW MORNING:

POCKET #2

5:20 AM
5:40 AM
REFLECT

COMPLETED: YES ☐ NO ☐

COMMITMENT FOR TOMORROW MORNING:

POCKET #3

5:40 AM
6:00 AM
GROW

COMPLETED: YES ☐ NO ☐

COMMITMENT FOR TOMORROW MORNING:

MORNING PRACTICE

5 MICRO GOALS FOR TODAY:

1.
2.
3.
4.
5.

EVENING PRACTICE

3 TINY WINS OF THIS DAY:

1.
2.
3.

PRE-SLEEP RITUAL DONE: YES ☐ NO ☐

"Discipline is built by consistently performing small acts of courage."

-ROBIN SHARMA-

MY DAILY REFLECTION

DAY 33/90

— THE 20/20/20 FORMULA™ —

POCKET #1

5:00 AM
5:20 AM
MOVE

COMPLETED: YES ☐ NO ☐

COMMITMENT FOR TOMORROW MORNING:

POCKET #2

5:20 AM
5:40 AM
REFLECT

COMPLETED: YES ☐ NO ☐

COMMITMENT FOR TOMORROW MORNING:

POCKET #3

5:40 AM
6:00 AM
GROW

COMPLETED: YES ☐ NO ☐

COMMITMENT FOR TOMORROW MORNING:

MORNING PRACTICE

5 MICRO GOALS FOR TODAY:

1.
2.
3.
4.
5.

EVENING PRACTICE

3 TINY WINS OF THIS DAY:

1.
2.
3.

PRE-SLEEP RITUAL DONE: YES ☐ NO ☐

"Fill your brain with giant dreams so there's no space for petty pursuits."
-ROBIN SHARMA-

MY DAILY REFLECTION

DAY 34/90

— THE 20/20/20 FORMULA™ —

POCKET #1

5:00 AM – 5:20 AM
MOVE

COMPLETED: YES ☐ NO ☐

COMMITMENT FOR TOMORROW MORNING:

POCKET #2

5:20 AM – 5:40 AM
REFLECT

COMPLETED: YES ☐ NO ☐

COMMITMENT FOR TOMORROW MORNING:

POCKET #3

5:40 AM – 6:00 AM
GROW

COMPLETED: YES ☐ NO ☐

COMMITMENT FOR TOMORROW MORNING:

MORNING PRACTICE

5 MICRO GOALS FOR TODAY:

1.
2.
3.
4.
5.

EVENING PRACTICE

3 TINY WINS OF THIS DAY:

1.
2.
3.

PRE-SLEEP RITUAL DONE: YES ☐ NO ☐

"Every thought plants a seed to one of your actions. Every action, good or bad, will yield a consequence. The person who takes good steps every day, cannot help but reap a harvest of awesome results."

-ROBIN SHARMA-

MY DAILY REFLECTION

DAY 35/90

— THE 20/20/20 FORMULA™ —

POCKET #1

5:00 AM
5:20 AM
MOVE

COMPLETED: YES ☐ NO ☐

COMMITMENT FOR TOMORROW MORNING:

POCKET #2

5:20 AM
5:40 AM
REFLECT

COMPLETED: YES ☐ NO ☐

COMMITMENT FOR TOMORROW MORNING:

POCKET #3

5:40 AM
6:00 AM
GROW

COMPLETED: YES ☐ NO ☐

COMMITMENT FOR TOMORROW MORNING:

MORNING PRACTICE

5 MICRO GOALS FOR TODAY:

1.
2.
3.
4.
5.

EVENING PRACTICE

3 TINY WINS OF THIS DAY:

1.
2.
3.

PRE-SLEEP RITUAL DONE: YES ☐ NO ☐

"Greatness loves gratitude."
-ROBIN SHARMA-

MY DAILY REFLECTION

STRATEGIC WEEKLY REVIEW

WHAT WORKED WELL THIS WEEK?

WHAT NEEDS TO BE IMPROVED?

WHAT CAN I CELEBRATE MYSELF FOR?

To download *The Weekly Planning Blueprint [WPB]* that I use to build out my own weeks, go to: The5amClub.com/weeklyplanner

MY 3 MAIN PERSONAL GOALS FOR THE WEEK AHEAD:

1.

2.

3.

MY 3 MAIN WORK GOALS FOR THE WEEK AHEAD:

1.

2.

3.

GENERAL OPTIMIZATIONS FOR THE WEEK AHEAD:

1.

2.

3.

DAY 36/90

— THE 20/20/20 FORMULA™ —

POCKET #1

5:00 AM
–
5:20 AM
MOVE

COMPLETED: YES ☐ NO ☐

COMMITMENT FOR TOMORROW MORNING:

POCKET #2

5:20 AM
–
5:40 AM
REFLECT

COMPLETED: YES ☐ NO ☐

COMMITMENT FOR TOMORROW MORNING:

POCKET #3

5:40 AM
–
6:00 AM
GROW

COMPLETED: YES ☐ NO ☐

COMMITMENT FOR TOMORROW MORNING:

MORNING PRACTICE

5 MICRO GOALS FOR TODAY:

1.
2.
3.
4.
5.

EVENING PRACTICE

3 TINY WINS OF THIS DAY:

1.
2.
3.

PRE-SLEEP RITUAL DONE: YES ☐ NO ☐

"If people aren't laughing at your dreams, your dreams aren't big enough."
-ROBIN SHARMA-

MY DAILY REFLECTION

DAY 37/90

— THE 20/20/20 FORMULA™ —

POCKET #1

5:00 AM
5:20 AM
MOVE

COMPLETED: YES ☐ NO ☐

COMMITMENT FOR TOMORROW MORNING:

POCKET #2

5:20 AM
5:40 AM
REFLECT

COMPLETED: YES ☐ NO ☐

COMMITMENT FOR TOMORROW MORNING:

POCKET #3

5:40 AM
6:00 AM
GROW

COMPLETED: YES ☐ NO ☐

COMMITMENT FOR TOMORROW MORNING:

MORNING PRACTICE

5 MICRO GOALS FOR TODAY:

1.
2.
3.
4.
5.

EVENING PRACTICE

3 TINY WINS OF THIS DAY:

1.
2.
3.

PRE-SLEEP RITUAL DONE: YES ☐ NO ☐

"Please remember: amazing takes time. And legendary requires patience."
-ROBIN SHARMA-

MY DAILY REFLECTION

DAY 38/90

— THE 20/20/20 FORMULA™ —

POCKET #1

5:00 AM
5:20 AM
MOVE

COMPLETED: YES ☐ NO ☐

COMMITMENT FOR TOMORROW MORNING:

POCKET #2

5:20 AM
5:40 AM
REFLECT

COMPLETED: YES ☐ NO ☐

COMMITMENT FOR TOMORROW MORNING:

POCKET #3

5:40 AM
6:00 AM
GROW

COMPLETED: YES ☐ NO ☐

COMMITMENT FOR TOMORROW MORNING:

MORNING PRACTICE

5 MICRO GOALS FOR TODAY:

1.
2.
3.
4.
5.

EVENING PRACTICE

3 TINY WINS OF THIS DAY:

1.
2.
3.

PRE-SLEEP RITUAL DONE: YES ☐ NO ☐

"The humblest is the greatest. The best listener is the most powerful person in the room. The most selfless always wins."

-ROBIN SHARMA-

MY DAILY REFLECTION

DAY 39/90

— THE 20/20/20 FORMULA™ —

POCKET #1

5:00 AM
–
5:20 AM
MOVE

COMPLETED: YES ☐ NO ☐

COMMITMENT FOR TOMORROW MORNING:

POCKET #2

5:20 AM
–
5:40 AM
REFLECT

COMPLETED: YES ☐ NO ☐

COMMITMENT FOR TOMORROW MORNING:

POCKET #3

5:40 AM
–
6:00 AM
GROW

COMPLETED: YES ☐ NO ☐

COMMITMENT FOR TOMORROW MORNING:

MORNING PRACTICE

5 MICRO GOALS FOR TODAY:

1.
2.
3.
4.
5.

EVENING PRACTICE

3 TINY WINS OF THIS DAY:

1.
2.
3.

PRE-SLEEP RITUAL DONE: YES ☐ NO ☐

"Life is short. Do big things."

-ROBIN SHARMA-

MY DAILY REFLECTION

DAY 40/90

— THE 20/20/20 FORMULA™ —

POCKET #1

5:00 AM
5:20 AM
MOVE

COMPLETED: YES ☐ NO ☐

COMMITMENT FOR TOMORROW MORNING:

POCKET #2

5:20 AM
5:40 AM
REFLECT

COMPLETED: YES ☐ NO ☐

COMMITMENT FOR TOMORROW MORNING:

POCKET #3

5:40 AM
6:00 AM
GROW

COMPLETED: YES ☐ NO ☐

COMMITMENT FOR TOMORROW MORNING:

MORNING PRACTICE

5 MICRO GOALS FOR TODAY:

1.
2.
3.
4.
5.

EVENING PRACTICE

3 TINY WINS OF THIS DAY:

1.
2.
3.

PRE-SLEEP RITUAL DONE: YES ☐ NO ☐

"The secret of epic performers is their daily rituals."
- ROBIN SHARMA -

MY DAILY REFLECTION

DAY 41/90

— THE 20/20/20 FORMULA™ —

POCKET #1

5:00 AM – 5:20 AM
MOVE

COMPLETED: YES ☐ NO ☐

COMMITMENT FOR TOMORROW MORNING:

POCKET #2

5:20 AM – 5:40 AM
REFLECT

COMPLETED: YES ☐ NO ☐

COMMITMENT FOR TOMORROW MORNING:

POCKET #3

5:40 AM – 6:00 AM
GROW

COMPLETED: YES ☐ NO ☐

COMMITMENT FOR TOMORROW MORNING:

MORNING PRACTICE

5 MICRO GOALS FOR TODAY:

1.
2.
3.
4.
5.

EVENING PRACTICE

3 TINY WINS OF THIS DAY:

1.
2.
3.

PRE-SLEEP RITUAL DONE: YES ☐ NO ☐

"This very day can be the first day of your new life."

-ROBIN SHARMA-

MY DAILY REFLECTION

DAY 42/90

— THE 20/20/20 FORMULA™ —

POCKET #1

5:00 AM – 5:20 AM
MOVE

COMPLETED: YES ☐ NO ☐

COMMITMENT FOR TOMORROW MORNING:

POCKET #2

5:20 AM – 5:40 AM
REFLECT

COMPLETED: YES ☐ NO ☐

COMMITMENT FOR TOMORROW MORNING:

POCKET #3

5:40 AM – 6:00 AM
GROW

COMPLETED: YES ☐ NO ☐

COMMITMENT FOR TOMORROW MORNING:

MORNING PRACTICE

5 MICRO GOALS FOR TODAY:

1.
2.
3.
4.
5.

EVENING PRACTICE

3 TINY WINS OF THIS DAY:

1.
2.
3.

PRE-SLEEP RITUAL DONE: YES ☐ NO ☐

"To lead is to make sure your daily schedule reflects your deepest priorities."

-ROBIN SHARMA-

MY DAILY REFLECTION

STRATEGIC WEEKLY REVIEW

WHAT WORKED WELL THIS WEEK?

WHAT NEEDS TO BE IMPROVED?

WHAT CAN I CELEBRATE MYSELF FOR?

To download *The Weekly Planning Blueprint [WPB]* that I use to build out my own weeks, go to: The5amClub.com/weeklyplanner

MY 3 MAIN PERSONAL GOALS FOR THE WEEK AHEAD:

1
2
3

MY 3 MAIN WORK GOALS FOR THE WEEK AHEAD:

1
2
3

GENERAL OPTIMIZATIONS FOR THE WEEK AHEAD:

1
2
3

DAY 43/90

— THE 20/20/20 FORMULA™ —

POCKET #1

5:00 AM
—
5:20 AM
MOVE

COMPLETED: YES ☐ NO ☐

COMMITMENT FOR TOMORROW MORNING:

POCKET #2

5:20 AM
—
5:40 AM
REFLECT

COMPLETED: YES ☐ NO ☐

COMMITMENT FOR TOMORROW MORNING:

POCKET #3

5:40 AM
—
6:00 AM
GROW

COMPLETED: YES ☐ NO ☐

COMMITMENT FOR TOMORROW MORNING:

MORNING PRACTICE

5 MICRO GOALS FOR TODAY:

1.
2.
3.
4.
5.

EVENING PRACTICE

3 TINY WINS OF THIS DAY:

1.
2.
3.

PRE-SLEEP RITUAL DONE: YES ☐ NO ☐

"You can get to world-class, or you can make excuses.
You can't do both."

-ROBIN SHARMA-

MY DAILY REFLECTION

DAY 44/90

— THE 20/20/20 FORMULA™ —

POCKET #1

5:00 AM
5:20 AM
MOVE

COMPLETED: YES ☐ NO ☐

COMMITMENT FOR TOMORROW MORNING:

POCKET #2

5:20 AM
5:40 AM
REFLECT

COMPLETED: YES ☐ NO ☐

COMMITMENT FOR TOMORROW MORNING:

POCKET #3

5:40 AM
6:00 AM
GROW

COMPLETED: YES ☐ NO ☐

COMMITMENT FOR TOMORROW MORNING:

MORNING PRACTICE

5 MICRO GOALS FOR TODAY:

1.
2.
3.
4.
5.

EVENING PRACTICE

3 TINY WINS OF THIS DAY:

1.
2.
3.

PRE-SLEEP RITUAL DONE: YES ☐ NO ☐

"Your life right now is a result of your dominant thoughts and your daily actions."

-ROBIN SHARMA-

MY DAILY REFLECTION

DAY 45/90

— THE 20/20/20 FORMULA™ —

POCKET #1

5:00 AM – 5:20 AM
MOVE

COMPLETED: YES ☐ NO ☐

COMMITMENT FOR TOMORROW MORNING:

POCKET #2

5:20 AM – 5:40 AM
REFLECT

COMPLETED: YES ☐ NO ☐

COMMITMENT FOR TOMORROW MORNING:

POCKET #3

5:40 AM – 6:00 AM
GROW

COMPLETED: YES ☐ NO ☐

COMMITMENT FOR TOMORROW MORNING:

MORNING PRACTICE

5 MICRO GOALS FOR TODAY:

1.
2.
3.
4.
5.

EVENING PRACTICE

3 TINY WINS OF THIS DAY:

1.
2.
3.

PRE-SLEEP RITUAL DONE: YES ☐ NO ☐

"Have the guts to be true to yourself. Nothing more."

-ROBIN SHARMA-

MY DAILY REFLECTION

DAY 46/90

— THE 20/20/20 FORMULA™ —

POCKET #1

5:00 AM
–
5:20 AM
MOVE

COMPLETED: YES ☐ NO ☐

COMMITMENT FOR TOMORROW MORNING:

POCKET #2

5:20 AM
–
5:40 AM
REFLECT

COMPLETED: YES ☐ NO ☐

COMMITMENT FOR TOMORROW MORNING:

POCKET #3

5:40 AM
–
6:00 AM
GROW

COMPLETED: YES ☐ NO ☐

COMMITMENT FOR TOMORROW MORNING:

MORNING PRACTICE

5 MICRO GOALS FOR TODAY:

1.
2.
3.
4.
5.

EVENING PRACTICE

3 TINY WINS OF THIS DAY:

1.
2.
3.

PRE-SLEEP RITUAL DONE: YES ☐ NO ☐

"Your habits are driving your performance.
Your rituals are creating your results."

-ROBIN SHARMA-

MY DAILY REFLECTION

DAY 47/90

— THE 20/20/20 FORMULA™ —

POCKET #1

5:00 AM – 5:20 AM
MOVE

COMPLETED: YES ☐ NO ☐

COMMITMENT FOR TOMORROW MORNING:

POCKET #2

5:20 AM – 5:40 AM
REFLECT

COMPLETED: YES ☐ NO ☐

COMMITMENT FOR TOMORROW MORNING:

POCKET #3

5:40 AM – 6:00 AM
GROW

COMPLETED: YES ☐ NO ☐

COMMITMENT FOR TOMORROW MORNING:

MORNING PRACTICE

5 MICRO GOALS FOR TODAY:

1.
2.
3.
4.
5.

EVENING PRACTICE

3 TINY WINS OF THIS DAY:

1.
2.
3.

PRE-SLEEP RITUAL DONE: YES ☐ NO ☐

"Optimize the basics. Complexity destroys world-class."

-ROBIN SHARMA-

MY DAILY REFLECTION

DAY 48/90

— THE 20/20/20 FORMULA™ —

POCKET #1

5:00 AM
5:20 AM
MOVE

COMPLETED: YES ☐ NO ☐

COMMITMENT FOR TOMORROW MORNING:

POCKET #2

5:20 AM
5:40 AM
REFLECT

COMPLETED: YES ☐ NO ☐

COMMITMENT FOR TOMORROW MORNING:

POCKET #3

5:40 AM
6:00 AM
GROW

COMPLETED: YES ☐ NO ☐

COMMITMENT FOR TOMORROW MORNING:

MORNING PRACTICE

5 MICRO GOALS FOR TODAY:

1.
2.
3.
4.
5.

EVENING PRACTICE

3 TINY WINS OF THIS DAY:

1.
2.
3.

PRE-SLEEP RITUAL DONE: YES ☐ NO ☐

"The marketplace rewards mastery. People always pay for the best."

-ROBIN SHARMA-

MY DAILY REFLECTION

DAY 49/90

— THE 20/20/20 FORMULA™ —

POCKET #1

5:00 AM
5:20 AM
MOVE

COMPLETED: YES ☐ NO ☐

COMMITMENT FOR TOMORROW MORNING:

POCKET #2

5:20 AM
5:40 AM
REFLECT

COMPLETED: YES ☐ NO ☐

COMMITMENT FOR TOMORROW MORNING:

POCKET #3

5:40 AM
6:00 AM
GROW

COMPLETED: YES ☐ NO ☐

COMMITMENT FOR TOMORROW MORNING:

MORNING PRACTICE

5 MICRO GOALS FOR TODAY:

1.
2.
3.
4.
5.

EVENING PRACTICE

3 TINY WINS OF THIS DAY:

1.
2.
3.

PRE-SLEEP RITUAL DONE: YES ☐ NO ☐

"Your results are dependent on your devotion.
Your performance reveals your practice."

- ROBIN SHARMA -

MY DAILY REFLECTION

STRATEGIC WEEKLY REVIEW

WHAT WORKED WELL THIS WEEK?

WHAT NEEDS TO BE IMPROVED?

WHAT CAN I CELEBRATE MYSELF FOR?

To download *The Weekly Planning Blueprint [WPB]* that I use to build out my own weeks, go to: The5amClub.com/weeklyplanner

MY 3 MAIN PERSONAL GOALS FOR THE WEEK AHEAD:

1

2

3

MY 3 MAIN WORK GOALS FOR THE WEEK AHEAD:

1

2

3

GENERAL OPTIMIZATIONS FOR THE WEEK AHEAD:

1

2

3

DAY 50/90

— THE 20/20/20 FORMULA™ —

POCKET #1

5:00 AM
—
5:20 AM
MOVE

COMPLETED: YES ☐ NO ☐

COMMITMENT FOR TOMORROW MORNING:

POCKET #2

5:20 AM
—
5:40 AM
REFLECT

COMPLETED: YES ☐ NO ☐

COMMITMENT FOR TOMORROW MORNING:

POCKET #3

5:40 AM
—
6:00 AM
GROW

COMPLETED: YES ☐ NO ☐

COMMITMENT FOR TOMORROW MORNING:

MORNING PRACTICE

5 MICRO GOALS FOR TODAY:

1.
2.
3.
4.
5.

EVENING PRACTICE

3 TINY WINS OF THIS DAY:

1.
2.
3.

PRE-SLEEP RITUAL DONE: YES ☐ NO ☐

"Be so good at what you do, we can't take our eyes off of you."

-ROBIN SHARMA-

MY DAILY REFLECTION

DAY 51/90

— THE 20/20/20 FORMULA™ —

POCKET #1

5:00 AM
–
5:20 AM
MOVE

COMPLETED: YES ☐ NO ☐

COMMITMENT FOR TOMORROW MORNING:

POCKET #2

5:20 AM
–
5:40 AM
REFLECT

COMPLETED: YES ☐ NO ☐

COMMITMENT FOR TOMORROW MORNING:

POCKET #3

5:40 AM
–
6:00 AM
GROW

COMPLETED: YES ☐ NO ☐

COMMITMENT FOR TOMORROW MORNING:

MORNING PRACTICE

5 MICRO GOALS FOR TODAY:

1.
2.
3.
4.
5.

EVENING PRACTICE

3 TINY WINS OF THIS DAY:

1.
2.
3.

PRE-SLEEP RITUAL DONE: YES ☐ NO ☐

"Be viscerally on fire to bring value to a massive number of people. The one who helps the most, wins."

-ROBIN SHARMA-

MY DAILY REFLECTION

DAY 52/90

— THE 20/20/20 FORMULA™ —

POCKET #1

5:00 AM
5:20 AM
MOVE

COMPLETED: YES ☐ NO ☐

COMMITMENT FOR TOMORROW MORNING:

POCKET #2

5:20 AM
5:40 AM
REFLECT

COMPLETED: YES ☐ NO ☐

COMMITMENT FOR TOMORROW MORNING:

POCKET #3

5:40 AM
6:00 AM
GROW

COMPLETED: YES ☐ NO ☐

COMMITMENT FOR TOMORROW MORNING:

MORNING PRACTICE

5 MICRO GOALS FOR TODAY:

1.
2.
3.
4.
5.

EVENING PRACTICE

3 TINY WINS OF THIS DAY:

1.
2.
3.

PRE-SLEEP RITUAL DONE: YES ☐ NO ☐

"Excuses don't construct monuments. Action does."

-ROBIN SHARMA-

MY DAILY REFLECTION

DAY 53/90

— THE 20/20/20 FORMULA™ —

POCKET #1

5:00 AM
5:20 AM
MOVE

COMPLETED: YES ☐ NO ☐

COMMITMENT FOR TOMORROW MORNING:

POCKET #2

5:20 AM
5:40 AM
REFLECT

COMPLETED: YES ☐ NO ☐

COMMITMENT FOR TOMORROW MORNING:

POCKET #3

5:40 AM
6:00 AM
GROW

COMPLETED: YES ☐ NO ☐

COMMITMENT FOR TOMORROW MORNING:

MORNING PRACTICE

5 MICRO GOALS FOR TODAY:

1.
2.
3.
4.
5.

EVENING PRACTICE

3 TINY WINS OF THIS DAY:

1.
2.
3.

PRE-SLEEP RITUAL DONE: YES ☐ NO ☐

"The great victory of success is being true to the grandest vision of your biggest life."

-ROBIN SHARMA-

MY DAILY REFLECTION

DAY 54/90

— THE 20/20/20 FORMULA™ —

POCKET #1

5:00 AM – 5:20 AM
MOVE

COMPLETED: YES ☐ NO ☐

COMMITMENT FOR TOMORROW MORNING:

POCKET #2

5:20 AM – 5:40 AM
REFLECT

COMPLETED: YES ☐ NO ☐

COMMITMENT FOR TOMORROW MORNING:

POCKET #3

5:40 AM – 6:00 AM
GROW

COMPLETED: YES ☐ NO ☐

COMMITMENT FOR TOMORROW MORNING:

MORNING PRACTICE

5 MICRO GOALS FOR TODAY:

1.
2.
3.
4.
5.

EVENING PRACTICE

3 TINY WINS OF THIS DAY:

1.
2.
3.

PRE-SLEEP RITUAL DONE: YES ☐ NO ☐

"As you grow more, you can see more.
As you know more, you can achieve more."

- ROBIN SHARMA -

MY DAILY REFLECTION

DAY 55/90

— THE 20/20/20 FORMULA™ —

POCKET #1

5:00 AM
—
5:20 AM
MOVE

COMPLETED: YES ☐ NO ☐

COMMITMENT FOR TOMORROW MORNING:

POCKET #2

5:20 AM
—
5:40 AM
REFLECT

COMPLETED: YES ☐ NO ☐

COMMITMENT FOR TOMORROW MORNING:

POCKET #3

5:40 AM
—
6:00 AM
GROW

COMPLETED: YES ☐ NO ☐

COMMITMENT FOR TOMORROW MORNING:

MORNING PRACTICE

5 MICRO GOALS FOR TODAY:

1.
2.
3.
4.
5.

EVENING PRACTICE

3 TINY WINS OF THIS DAY:

1.
2.
3.

PRE-SLEEP RITUAL DONE: YES ☐ NO ☐

"Ideas don't work without you doing the work."

-ROBIN SHARMA-

MY DAILY REFLECTION

DAY 56/90

— THE 20/20/20 FORMULA™ —

POCKET #1

5:00 AM
–
5:20 AM
MOVE

COMPLETED: YES ☐ NO ☐

COMMITMENT FOR TOMORROW MORNING:

POCKET #2

5:20 AM
–
5:40 AM
REFLECT

COMPLETED: YES ☐ NO ☐

COMMITMENT FOR TOMORROW MORNING:

POCKET #3

5:40 AM
–
6:00 AM
GROW

COMPLETED: YES ☐ NO ☐

COMMITMENT FOR TOMORROW MORNING:

MORNING PRACTICE

5 MICRO GOALS FOR TODAY:

1.
2.
3.
4.
5.

EVENING PRACTICE

3 TINY WINS OF THIS DAY:

1.
2.
3.

PRE-SLEEP RITUAL DONE: YES ☐ NO ☐

"Nothing happens until you move."

-ROBIN SHARMA-

MY DAILY REFLECTION

STRATEGIC WEEKLY REVIEW

WHAT WORKED WELL THIS WEEK?

WHAT NEEDS TO BE IMPROVED?

WHAT CAN I CELEBRATE MYSELF FOR?

To download *The Weekly Planning Blueprint [WPB]* that I use to build out my own weeks, go to: The5amClub.com/weeklyplanner

MY 3 MAIN PERSONAL GOALS FOR THE WEEK AHEAD:

1.
2.
3.

MY 3 MAIN WORK GOALS FOR THE WEEK AHEAD:

1.
2.
3.

GENERAL OPTIMIZATIONS FOR THE WEEK AHEAD:

1.
2.
3.

DAY 57/90

— THE 20/20/20 FORMULA™ —

POCKET #1

5:00 AM
5:20 AM
MOVE

COMPLETED: YES ☐ NO ☐

COMMITMENT FOR TOMORROW MORNING:

POCKET #2

5:20 AM
5:40 AM
REFLECT

COMPLETED: YES ☐ NO ☐

COMMITMENT FOR TOMORROW MORNING:

POCKET #3

5:40 AM
6:00 AM
GROW

COMPLETED: YES ☐ NO ☐

COMMITMENT FOR TOMORROW MORNING:

MORNING PRACTICE

5 MICRO GOALS FOR TODAY:

1.
2.
3.
4.
5.

EVENING PRACTICE

3 TINY WINS OF THIS DAY:

1.
2.
3.

PRE-SLEEP RITUAL DONE: YES ☐ NO ☐

"Beneath every excuse lies a fear. Practice being fearless."

-ROBIN SHARMA-

MY DAILY REFLECTION

DAY 58/90

— THE 20/20/20 FORMULA™ —

POCKET #1

5:00 AM – 5:20 AM
MOVE

COMPLETED: YES ☐ NO ☐

COMMITMENT FOR TOMORROW MORNING:

POCKET #2

5:20 AM – 5:40 AM
REFLECT

COMPLETED: YES ☐ NO ☐

COMMITMENT FOR TOMORROW MORNING:

POCKET #3

5:40 AM – 6:00 AM
GROW

COMPLETED: YES ☐ NO ☐

COMMITMENT FOR TOMORROW MORNING:

MORNING PRACTICE

5 MICRO GOALS FOR TODAY:

1.
2.
3.
4.
5.

EVENING PRACTICE

3 TINY WINS OF THIS DAY:

1.
2.
3.

PRE-SLEEP RITUAL DONE: YES ☐ NO ☐

"Sometimes you'll be the only one who believes in your dream. Do not stop. The world needs you to model what's possible for the rest of us."

-ROBIN SHARMA-

MY DAILY REFLECTION

DAY 59/90

— THE 20/20/20 FORMULA™ —

POCKET #1

5:00 AM – 5:20 AM
MOVE

COMPLETED: YES ☐ NO ☐

COMMITMENT FOR TOMORROW MORNING:

POCKET #2

5:20 AM – 5:40 AM
REFLECT

COMPLETED: YES ☐ NO ☐

COMMITMENT FOR TOMORROW MORNING:

POCKET #3

5:40 AM – 6:00 AM
GROW

COMPLETED: YES ☐ NO ☐

COMMITMENT FOR TOMORROW MORNING:

MORNING PRACTICE

5 MICRO GOALS FOR TODAY:

1.
2.
3.
4.
5.

EVENING PRACTICE

3 TINY WINS OF THIS DAY:

1.
2.
3.

PRE-SLEEP RITUAL DONE: YES ☐ NO ☐

"Become a master of time management."
-ROBIN SHARMA-

MY DAILY REFLECTION

DAY 60/90

— THE 20/20/20 FORMULA™ —

POCKET #1

5:00 AM
5:20 AM
MOVE

COMPLETED: YES ☐ NO ☐

COMMITMENT FOR TOMORROW MORNING:

POCKET #2

5:20 AM
5:40 AM
REFLECT

COMPLETED: YES ☐ NO ☐

COMMITMENT FOR TOMORROW MORNING:

POCKET #3

5:40 AM
6:00 AM
GROW

COMPLETED: YES ☐ NO ☐

COMMITMENT FOR TOMORROW MORNING:

MORNING PRACTICE
5 MICRO GOALS FOR TODAY:

1.
2.
3.
4.
5.

EVENING PRACTICE
3 TINY WINS OF THIS DAY:

1.
2.
3.

PRE-SLEEP RITUAL DONE: YES ☐ NO ☐

"Every minute spent worrying about 'the way things were' is a moment stolen from creating 'the way things can be.'"

- ROBIN SHARMA -

MY DAILY REFLECTION

30 DAY PERFORMANCE INQUIRY

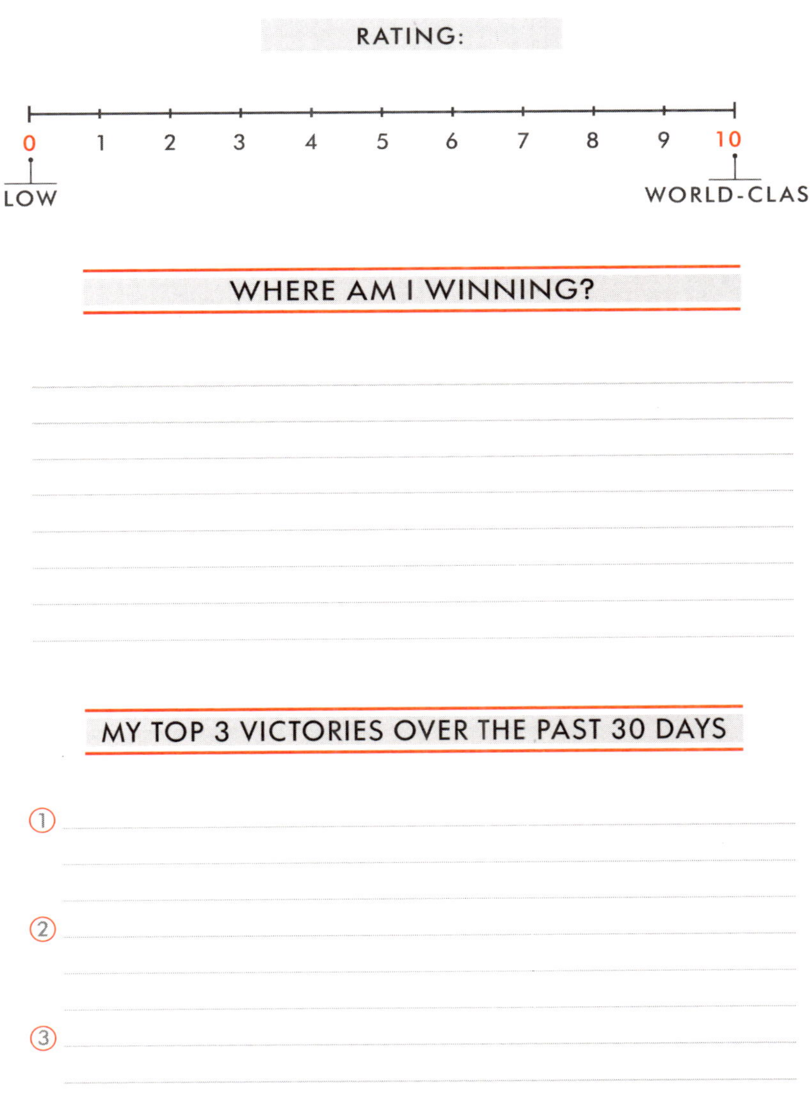

MY IDEAL NEXT 30 DAYS AS A DRAWING

5 PROGRESS ACCELERATORS THAT WILL MAKE THE NEXT 30 DAYS MY BEST 30 DAYS YET

1.

2.

3.

4.

5.

DAY 61/90

— THE 20/20/20 FORMULA™ —

POCKET #1

5:00 AM
–
5:20 AM
MOVE

COMPLETED: YES ☐ NO ☐

COMMITMENT FOR TOMORROW MORNING:

POCKET #2

5:20 AM
–
5:40 AM
REFLECT

COMPLETED: YES ☐ NO ☐

COMMITMENT FOR TOMORROW MORNING:

POCKET #3

5:40 AM
–
6:00 AM
GROW

COMPLETED: YES ☐ NO ☐

COMMITMENT FOR TOMORROW MORNING:

MORNING PRACTICE

5 MICRO GOALS FOR TODAY:

1.
2.
3.
4.
5.

EVENING PRACTICE

3 TINY WINS OF THIS DAY:

1.
2.
3.

PRE-SLEEP RITUAL DONE: YES ☐ NO ☐

"Wage a war against weakness and launch a campaign against fearlessness."

-ROBIN SHARMA-

MY DAILY REFLECTION

DAY 62/90

— THE 20/20/20 FORMULA™ —

POCKET #1

5:00 AM
–
5:20 AM
MOVE

COMPLETED: YES ☐ NO ☐

COMMITMENT FOR TOMORROW MORNING:

POCKET #2

5:20 AM
–
5:40 AM
REFLECT

COMPLETED: YES ☐ NO ☐

COMMITMENT FOR TOMORROW MORNING:

POCKET #3

5:40 AM
–
6:00 AM
GROW

COMPLETED: YES ☐ NO ☐

COMMITMENT FOR TOMORROW MORNING:

MORNING PRACTICE

5 MICRO GOALS FOR TODAY:

1.
2.
3.
4.
5.

EVENING PRACTICE

3 TINY WINS OF THIS DAY:

1.
2.
3.

PRE-SLEEP RITUAL DONE: YES ☐ NO ☐

"Journaling is meditating on paper."

-ROBIN SHARMA-

MY DAILY REFLECTION

DAY 63/90

— THE 20/20/20 FORMULA™ —

POCKET #1

5:00 AM
—
5:20 AM
MOVE

COMPLETED: YES ☐ NO ☐

COMMITMENT FOR TOMORROW MORNING:

POCKET #2

5:20 AM
—
5:40 AM
REFLECT

COMPLETED: YES ☐ NO ☐

COMMITMENT FOR TOMORROW MORNING:

POCKET #3

5:40 AM
—
6:00 AM
GROW

COMPLETED: YES ☐ NO ☐

COMMITMENT FOR TOMORROW MORNING:

MORNING PRACTICE
5 MICRO GOALS FOR TODAY:

1.
2.
3.
4.
5.

EVENING PRACTICE
3 TINY WINS OF THIS DAY:

1.
2.
3.

PRE-SLEEP RITUAL DONE: YES ☐ NO ☐

"Failure is fuel for success. If you choose so."

-ROBIN SHARMA-

MY DAILY REFLECTION

STRATEGIC WEEKLY REVIEW

WHAT WORKED WELL THIS WEEK?

WHAT NEEDS TO BE IMPROVED?

WHAT CAN I CELEBRATE MYSELF FOR?

To download *The Weekly Planning Blueprint [WPB]* that I use to build out my own weeks, go to: The5amClub.com/weeklyplanner

MY 3 MAIN PERSONAL GOALS FOR THE WEEK AHEAD:

1.

2.

3.

MY 3 MAIN WORK GOALS FOR THE WEEK AHEAD:

1.

2.

3.

GENERAL OPTIMIZATIONS FOR THE WEEK AHEAD:

1.

2.

3.

DAY 64/90

— THE 20/20/20 FORMULA™ —

POCKET #1

5:00 AM – 5:20 AM
MOVE

COMPLETED: YES ☐ NO ☐

COMMITMENT FOR TOMORROW MORNING:

POCKET #2

5:20 AM – 5:40 AM
REFLECT

COMPLETED: YES ☐ NO ☐

COMMITMENT FOR TOMORROW MORNING:

POCKET #3

5:40 AM – 6:00 AM
GROW

COMPLETED: YES ☐ NO ☐

COMMITMENT FOR TOMORROW MORNING:

MORNING PRACTICE

5 MICRO GOALS FOR TODAY:

1.
2.
3.
4.
5.

EVENING PRACTICE

3 TINY WINS OF THIS DAY:

1.
2.
3.

PRE-SLEEP RITUAL DONE: YES ☐ NO ☐

"Jealousy is the price of ambition. Obstacles are the cost of greatness."

-ROBIN SHARMA-

MY DAILY REFLECTION

DAY 65/90

— THE 20/20/20 FORMULA™ —

POCKET #1

5:00 AM
5:20 AM
MOVE

COMPLETED: YES ☐ NO ☐

COMMITMENT FOR TOMORROW MORNING:

POCKET #2

5:20 AM
5:40 AM
REFLECT

COMPLETED: YES ☐ NO ☐

COMMITMENT FOR TOMORROW MORNING:

POCKET #3

5:40 AM
6:00 AM
GROW

COMPLETED: YES ☐ NO ☐

COMMITMENT FOR TOMORROW MORNING:

MORNING PRACTICE

5 MICRO GOALS FOR TODAY:

1.
2.
3.
4.
5.

EVENING PRACTICE

3 TINY WINS OF THIS DAY:

1.
2.
3.

PRE-SLEEP RITUAL DONE: YES ☐ NO ☐

"The way you start your day determines how well you live your day."

-ROBIN SHARMA-

MY DAILY REFLECTION

DAY 66/90

— THE 20/20/20 FORMULA™ —

POCKET #1

5:00 AM
–
5:20 AM
MOVE

COMPLETED: YES ☐ NO ☐

COMMITMENT FOR TOMORROW MORNING:

POCKET #2

5:20 AM
–
5:40 AM
REFLECT

COMPLETED: YES ☐ NO ☐

COMMITMENT FOR TOMORROW MORNING:

POCKET #3

5:40 AM
–
6:00 AM
GROW

COMPLETED: YES ☐ NO ☐

COMMITMENT FOR TOMORROW MORNING:

MORNING PRACTICE

5 MICRO GOALS FOR TODAY:

1.
2.
3.
4.
5.

EVENING PRACTICE

3 TINY WINS OF THIS DAY:

1.
2.
3.

PRE-SLEEP RITUAL DONE: YES ☐ NO ☐

"Stop settling for 'good enough'. You deserve what's best."

-ROBIN SHARMA-

MY DAILY REFLECTION

DAY 67/90

— THE 20/20/20 FORMULA™ —

POCKET #1

5:00 AM – 5:20 AM
MOVE

COMPLETED: YES ☐ NO ☐

COMMITMENT FOR TOMORROW MORNING:

POCKET #2

5:20 AM – 5:40 AM
REFLECT

COMPLETED: YES ☐ NO ☐

COMMITMENT FOR TOMORROW MORNING:

POCKET #3

5:40 AM – 6:00 AM
GROW

COMPLETED: YES ☐ NO ☐

COMMITMENT FOR TOMORROW MORNING:

MORNING PRACTICE

5 MICRO GOALS FOR TODAY:

1.
2.
3.
4.
5.

EVENING PRACTICE

3 TINY WINS OF THIS DAY:

1.
2.
3.

PRE-SLEEP RITUAL DONE: YES ☐ NO ☐

"Simplicity is the trademark of genius."
-ROBIN SHARMA-

MY DAILY REFLECTION

DAY 68/90

— THE 20/20/20 FORMULA™ —

POCKET #1

5:00 AM
5:20 AM
MOVE

COMPLETED: YES ☐ NO ☐

COMMITMENT FOR TOMORROW MORNING:

POCKET #2

5:20 AM
5:40 AM
REFLECT

COMPLETED: YES ☐ NO ☐

COMMITMENT FOR TOMORROW MORNING:

POCKET #3

5:40 AM
6:00 AM
GROW

COMPLETED: YES ☐ NO ☐

COMMITMENT FOR TOMORROW MORNING:

MORNING PRACTICE

5 MICRO GOALS FOR TODAY:

1.
2.
3.
4.
5.

EVENING PRACTICE

3 TINY WINS OF THIS DAY:

1.
2.
3.

PRE-SLEEP RITUAL DONE: YES ☐ NO ☐

"Never miss a chance to be kind."
-ROBIN SHARMA-

MY DAILY REFLECTION

DAY 69/90

— THE 20/20/20 FORMULA™ —

POCKET #1

5:00 AM
5:20 AM
MOVE

COMPLETED: YES ☐ NO ☐

COMMITMENT FOR TOMORROW MORNING:

POCKET #2

5:20 AM
5:40 AM
REFLECT

COMPLETED: YES ☐ NO ☐

COMMITMENT FOR TOMORROW MORNING:

POCKET #3

5:40 AM
6:00 AM
GROW

COMPLETED: YES ☐ NO ☐

COMMITMENT FOR TOMORROW MORNING:

MORNING PRACTICE

5 MICRO GOALS FOR TODAY:

1.
2.
3.
4.
5.

EVENING PRACTICE

3 TINY WINS OF THIS DAY:

1.
2.
3.

PRE-SLEEP RITUAL DONE: YES ☐ NO ☐

"The truth is that every challenging event you've experienced, each toxic person that you've encountered and all the trials you've endured have been the perfect preparation to make you the person that you are now."

-ROBIN SHARMA-

MY DAILY REFLECTION

DAY 70/90

— THE 20/20/20 FORMULA™ —

POCKET #1

5:00 AM
–
5:20 AM
MOVE

COMPLETED: YES ☐ NO ☐

COMMITMENT FOR TOMORROW MORNING:

POCKET #2

5:20 AM
–
5:40 AM
REFLECT

COMPLETED: YES ☐ NO ☐

COMMITMENT FOR TOMORROW MORNING:

POCKET #3

5:40 AM
–
6:00 AM
GROW

COMPLETED: YES ☐ NO ☐

COMMITMENT FOR TOMORROW MORNING:

MORNING PRACTICE

5 MICRO GOALS FOR TODAY:

1.
2.
3.
4.
5.

EVENING PRACTICE

3 TINY WINS OF THIS DAY:

1.
2.
3.

PRE-SLEEP RITUAL DONE: YES ☐ NO ☐

"You've been built to achieve masterwork-level projects, designed to realize unusually important pursuits and constructed to be a force for good on this tiny planet."

-ROBIN SHARMA-

MY DAILY REFLECTION

STRATEGIC WEEKLY REVIEW

WHAT WORKED WELL THIS WEEK?

WHAT NEEDS TO BE IMPROVED?

WHAT CAN I CELEBRATE MYSELF FOR?

To download *The Weekly Planning Blueprint [WPB]* that I use to build out my own weeks, go to: The5amClub.com/weeklyplanner

MY 3 MAIN PERSONAL GOALS FOR THE WEEK AHEAD:

1.
2.
3.

MY 3 MAIN WORK GOALS FOR THE WEEK AHEAD:

1.
2.
3.

GENERAL OPTIMIZATIONS FOR THE WEEK AHEAD:

1.
2.
3.

DAY 71/90

— THE 20/20/20 FORMULA™ —

POCKET #1

5:00 AM
–
5:20 AM
MOVE

COMPLETED: YES ☐ NO ☐

COMMITMENT FOR TOMORROW MORNING:

POCKET #2

5:20 AM
–
5:40 AM
REFLECT

COMPLETED: YES ☐ NO ☐

COMMITMENT FOR TOMORROW MORNING:

POCKET #3

5:40 AM
–
6:00 AM
GROW

COMPLETED: YES ☐ NO ☐

COMMITMENT FOR TOMORROW MORNING:

MORNING PRACTICE

5 MICRO GOALS FOR TODAY:

1.
2.
3.
4.
5.

EVENING PRACTICE

3 TINY WINS OF THIS DAY:

1.
2.
3.

PRE-SLEEP RITUAL DONE: YES ☐ NO ☐

"Ordinary people can accomplish extraordinary feats, once they've routinized the right habits."

-ROBIN SHARMA-

MY DAILY REFLECTION

DAY 72/90

— THE 20/20/20 FORMULA™ —

POCKET #1

5:00 AM
5:20 AM
MOVE

COMPLETED: YES ☐ NO ☐

COMMITMENT FOR TOMORROW MORNING:

POCKET #2

5:20 AM
5:40 AM
REFLECT

COMPLETED: YES ☐ NO ☐

COMMITMENT FOR TOMORROW MORNING:

POCKET #3

5:40 AM
6:00 AM
GROW

COMPLETED: YES ☐ NO ☐

COMMITMENT FOR TOMORROW MORNING:

MORNING PRACTICE

5 MICRO GOALS FOR TODAY:

1.
2.
3.
4.
5.

EVENING PRACTICE

3 TINY WINS OF THIS DAY:

1.
2.
3.

PRE-SLEEP RITUAL DONE: YES ☐ NO ☐

"A genius is just a producer who didn't stop studying, kept on practising and refused to become distracted."

- ROBIN SHARMA -

MY DAILY REFLECTION

DAY 73/90

— THE 20/20/20 FORMULA™ —

POCKET #1

5:00 AM
5:20 AM
MOVE

COMPLETED: YES ☐ NO ☐

COMMITMENT FOR TOMORROW MORNING:

POCKET #2

5:20 AM
5:40 AM
REFLECT

COMPLETED: YES ☐ NO ☐

COMMITMENT FOR TOMORROW MORNING:

POCKET #3

5:40 AM
6:00 AM
GROW

COMPLETED: YES ☐ NO ☐

COMMITMENT FOR TOMORROW MORNING:

MORNING PRACTICE

5 MICRO GOALS FOR TODAY:

1.
2.
3.
4.
5.

EVENING PRACTICE

3 TINY WINS OF THIS DAY:

1.
2.
3.

PRE-SLEEP RITUAL DONE: YES ☐ NO ☐

"Everything is created twice, first in the mind and then in reality."

-ROBIN SHARMA-

MY DAILY REFLECTION

DAY 74/90

— THE 20/20/20 FORMULA™ —

POCKET #1

5:00 AM
5:20 AM
MOVE

COMPLETED: YES ☐ NO ☐

COMMITMENT FOR TOMORROW MORNING:

POCKET #2

5:20 AM
5:40 AM
REFLECT

COMPLETED: YES ☐ NO ☐

COMMITMENT FOR TOMORROW MORNING:

POCKET #3

5:40 AM
6:00 AM
GROW

COMPLETED: YES ☐ NO ☐

COMMITMENT FOR TOMORROW MORNING:

MORNING PRACTICE

5 MICRO GOALS FOR TODAY:

1.
2.
3.
4.
5.

EVENING PRACTICE

3 TINY WINS OF THIS DAY:

1.
2.
3.

PRE-SLEEP RITUAL DONE: YES ☐ NO ☐

"Never lose hope. Unexpected blessings are coming your way."

-ROBIN SHARMA-

MY DAILY REFLECTION

DAY 75/90

— THE 20/20/20 FORMULA™ —

POCKET #1

5:00 AM
5:20 AM
MOVE

COMPLETED: YES ☐ NO ☐

COMMITMENT FOR TOMORROW MORNING:

POCKET #2

5:20 AM
5:40 AM
REFLECT

COMPLETED: YES ☐ NO ☐

COMMITMENT FOR TOMORROW MORNING:

POCKET #3

5:40 AM
6:00 AM
GROW

COMPLETED: YES ☐ NO ☐

COMMITMENT FOR TOMORROW MORNING:

MORNING PRACTICE

5 MICRO GOALS FOR TODAY:

1.
2.
3.
4.
5.

EVENING PRACTICE

3 TINY WINS OF THIS DAY:

1.
2.
3.

PRE-SLEEP RITUAL DONE: YES ☐ NO ☐

"The great thing about a master is that they never think they are a master."
-ROBIN SHARMA-

MY DAILY REFLECTION

DAY 76/90

— THE 20/20/20 FORMULA™ —

POCKET #1

5:00 AM
—
5:20 AM
MOVE

COMPLETED: YES ☐ NO ☐

COMMITMENT FOR TOMORROW MORNING:

POCKET #2

5:20 AM
—
5:40 AM
REFLECT

COMPLETED: YES ☐ NO ☐

COMMITMENT FOR TOMORROW MORNING:

POCKET #3

5:40 AM
—
6:00 AM
GROW

COMPLETED: YES ☐ NO ☐

COMMITMENT FOR TOMORROW MORNING:

MORNING PRACTICE

5 MICRO GOALS FOR TODAY:

1.
2.
3.
4.
5.

EVENING PRACTICE

3 TINY WINS OF THIS DAY:

1.
2.
3.

PRE-SLEEP RITUAL DONE: YES ☐ NO ☐

"Finish the symphony. Deliver the poetry. Exile from mediocrity. Confess your majesty. Rise to legendary."

-ROBIN SHARMA-

MY DAILY REFLECTION

DAY 77/90

— THE 20/20/20 FORMULA™ —

POCKET #1

5:00 AM
5:20 AM
MOVE

COMPLETED: YES ☐ NO ☐

COMMITMENT FOR TOMORROW MORNING:

POCKET #2

5:20 AM
5:40 AM
REFLECT

COMPLETED: YES ☐ NO ☐

COMMITMENT FOR TOMORROW MORNING:

POCKET #3

5:40 AM
6:00 AM
GROW

COMPLETED: YES ☐ NO ☐

COMMITMENT FOR TOMORROW MORNING:

MORNING PRACTICE

5 MICRO GOALS FOR TODAY:

1.
2.
3.
4.
5.

EVENING PRACTICE

3 TINY WINS OF THIS DAY:

1.
2.
3.

PRE-SLEEP RITUAL DONE: YES ☐ NO ☐

"Stop being a prisoner of your past. Become the architect of your future."

-ROBIN SHARMA-

MY DAILY REFLECTION

STRATEGIC WEEKLY REVIEW

WHAT WORKED WELL THIS WEEK?

WHAT NEEDS TO BE IMPROVED?

WHAT CAN I CELEBRATE MYSELF FOR?

To download *The Weekly Planning Blueprint [WPB]* that I use to build out my own weeks, go to: The5amClub.com/weeklyplanner

MY 3 MAIN PERSONAL GOALS FOR THE WEEK AHEAD:

1.

2.

3.

MY 3 MAIN WORK GOALS FOR THE WEEK AHEAD:

1.

2.

3.

GENERAL OPTIMIZATIONS FOR THE WEEK AHEAD:

1.

2.

3.

DAY 78/90

— THE 20/20/20 FORMULA™ —

POCKET #1

5:00 AM
–
5:20 AM
MOVE

COMPLETED: YES ☐ NO ☐

COMMITMENT FOR TOMORROW MORNING:

POCKET #2

5:20 AM
–
5:40 AM
REFLECT

COMPLETED: YES ☐ NO ☐

COMMITMENT FOR TOMORROW MORNING:

POCKET #3

5:40 AM
–
6:00 AM
GROW

COMPLETED: YES ☐ NO ☐

COMMITMENT FOR TOMORROW MORNING:

MORNING PRACTICE

5 MICRO GOALS FOR TODAY:

1.
2.
3.
4.
5.

EVENING PRACTICE

3 TINY WINS OF THIS DAY:

1.
2.
3.

PRE-SLEEP RITUAL DONE: YES ☐ NO ☐

"Wage a war against weakness and launch a campaign against fearfulness. You truly can get up early. And doing so is a necessity in your awesome pursuit toward legendary."

-ROBIN SHARMA-

MY DAILY REFLECTION

DAY 79/90

— THE 20/20/20 FORMULA™ —

POCKET #1

5:00 AM
5:20 AM
MOVE

COMPLETED: YES ☐ NO ☐

COMMITMENT FOR TOMORROW MORNING:

POCKET #2

5:20 AM
5:40 AM
REFLECT

COMPLETED: YES ☐ NO ☐

COMMITMENT FOR TOMORROW MORNING:

POCKET #3

5:40 AM
6:00 AM
GROW

COMPLETED: YES ☐ NO ☐

COMMITMENT FOR TOMORROW MORNING:

MORNING PRACTICE

5 MICRO GOALS FOR TODAY:

1.
2.
3.
4.
5.

EVENING PRACTICE

3 TINY WINS OF THIS DAY:

1.
2.
3.

PRE-SLEEP RITUAL DONE: YES ☐ NO ☐

"If world-class was easy, everyone would be doing it."

-ROBIN SHARMA-

MY DAILY REFLECTION

DAY 80/90

— THE 20/20/20 FORMULA™ —

POCKET #1

5:00 AM
—
5:20 AM
MOVE

COMPLETED: YES ☐ NO ☐

COMMITMENT FOR TOMORROW MORNING:

POCKET #2

5:20 AM
—
5:40 AM
REFLECT

COMPLETED: YES ☐ NO ☐

COMMITMENT FOR TOMORROW MORNING:

POCKET #3

5:40 AM
—
6:00 AM
GROW

COMPLETED: YES ☐ NO ☐

COMMITMENT FOR TOMORROW MORNING:

MORNING PRACTICE

5 MICRO GOALS FOR TODAY:

1.
2.
3.
4.
5.

EVENING PRACTICE

3 TINY WINS OF THIS DAY:

1.
2.
3.

PRE-SLEEP RITUAL DONE: YES ☐ NO ☐

"Growth is the real sport that the best play, every day."

-ROBIN SHARMA-

MY DAILY REFLECTION

DAY 81/90

— THE 20/20/20 FORMULA™ —

POCKET #1

5:00 AM
–
5:20 AM
MOVE

COMPLETED: YES ☐ NO ☐

COMMITMENT FOR TOMORROW MORNING:

POCKET #2

5:20 AM
–
5:40 AM
REFLECT

COMPLETED: YES ☐ NO ☐

COMMITMENT FOR TOMORROW MORNING:

POCKET #3

5:40 AM
–
6:00 AM
GROW

COMPLETED: YES ☐ NO ☐

COMMITMENT FOR TOMORROW MORNING:

MORNING PRACTICE

5 MICRO GOALS FOR TODAY:

1.
2.
3.
4.
5.

EVENING PRACTICE

3 TINY WINS OF THIS DAY:

1.
2.
3.

PRE-SLEEP RITUAL DONE: YES ☐ NO ☐

"Become the hero the world is waiting for you to be.
A long life is a short ride."

-ROBIN SHARMA-

MY DAILY REFLECTION

DAY 82/90

— THE 20/20/20 FORMULA™ —

POCKET #1

5:00 AM
5:20 AM
MOVE

COMPLETED: YES ☐ NO ☐

COMMITMENT FOR TOMORROW MORNING:

POCKET #2

5:20 AM
5:40 AM
REFLECT

COMPLETED: YES ☐ NO ☐

COMMITMENT FOR TOMORROW MORNING:

POCKET #3

5:40 AM
6:00 AM
GROW

COMPLETED: YES ☐ NO ☐

COMMITMENT FOR TOMORROW MORNING:

MORNING PRACTICE

5 MICRO GOALS FOR TODAY:

1.
2.
3.
4.
5.

EVENING PRACTICE

3 TINY WINS OF THIS DAY:

1.
2.
3.

PRE-SLEEP RITUAL DONE: YES ☐ NO ☐

"Turn pain into power, limitation into leadership, horror into hope and busy into productivity."

- ROBIN SHARMA -

MY DAILY REFLECTION

DAY 83/90

— THE 20/20/20 FORMULA™ —

POCKET #1

5:00 AM
5:20 AM
MOVE

COMPLETED: YES ☐ NO ☐

COMMITMENT FOR TOMORROW MORNING:

POCKET #2

5:20 AM
5:40 AM
REFLECT

COMPLETED: YES ☐ NO ☐

COMMITMENT FOR TOMORROW MORNING:

POCKET #3

5:40 AM
6:00 AM
GROW

COMPLETED: YES ☐ NO ☐

COMMITMENT FOR TOMORROW MORNING:

MORNING PRACTICE

5 MICRO GOALS FOR TODAY:

1.
2.
3.
4.
5.

EVENING PRACTICE

3 TINY WINS OF THIS DAY:

1.
2.
3.

PRE-SLEEP RITUAL DONE: YES ☐ NO ☐

"Elite performance without magnificent renewal leads to depletion of your genius. Take the time to rest, read, think, love, learn and have big fun."

-ROBIN SHARMA-

MY DAILY REFLECTION

DAY 84/90

— THE 20/20/20 FORMULA™ —

POCKET #1

5:00 AM – 5:20 AM
MOVE

COMPLETED: YES ☐ NO ☐

COMMITMENT FOR TOMORROW MORNING:

POCKET #2

5:20 AM – 5:40 AM
REFLECT

COMPLETED: YES ☐ NO ☐

COMMITMENT FOR TOMORROW MORNING:

POCKET #3

5:40 AM – 6:00 AM
GROW

COMPLETED: YES ☐ NO ☐

COMMITMENT FOR TOMORROW MORNING:

MORNING PRACTICE

5 MICRO GOALS FOR TODAY:

1.
2.
3.
4.
5.

EVENING PRACTICE

3 TINY WINS OF THIS DAY:

1.
2.
3.

PRE-SLEEP RITUAL DONE: YES ☐ NO ☐

"Cost matters less than the rewards you'll gain from your investment."

-ROBIN SHARMA-

MY DAILY REFLECTION

STRATEGIC WEEKLY REVIEW

WHAT WORKED WELL THIS WEEK?

WHAT NEEDS TO BE IMPROVED?

WHAT CAN I CELEBRATE MYSELF FOR?

To download *The Weekly Planning Blueprint [WPB]* that I use to build out my own weeks, go to: The5amClub.com/weeklyplanner

MY 3 MAIN PERSONAL GOALS FOR THE WEEK AHEAD:

1

2

3

MY 3 MAIN WORK GOALS FOR THE WEEK AHEAD:

1

2

3

GENERAL OPTIMIZATIONS FOR THE WEEK AHEAD:

1

2

3

DAY 85/90

— THE 20/20/20 FORMULA™ —

POCKET #1

5:00 AM
5:20 AM
MOVE

COMPLETED: YES ☐ NO ☐

COMMITMENT FOR TOMORROW MORNING:

POCKET #2

5:20 AM
5:40 AM
REFLECT

COMPLETED: YES ☐ NO ☐

COMMITMENT FOR TOMORROW MORNING:

POCKET #3

5:40 AM
6:00 AM
GROW

COMPLETED: YES ☐ NO ☐

COMMITMENT FOR TOMORROW MORNING:

MORNING PRACTICE

5 MICRO GOALS FOR TODAY:

1.
2.
3.
4.
5.

EVENING PRACTICE

3 TINY WINS OF THIS DAY:

1.
2.
3.

PRE-SLEEP RITUAL DONE: YES ☐ NO ☐

"To double your net worth, double your self-worth. Because you will never exceed the height of your self-image."

- ROBIN SHARMA -

MY DAILY REFLECTION

DAY 86/90

— THE 20/20/20 FORMULA™ —

POCKET #1

5:00 AM
5:20 AM
MOVE

COMPLETED: YES ☐ NO ☐

COMMITMENT FOR TOMORROW MORNING:

POCKET #2

5:20 AM
5:40 AM
REFLECT

COMPLETED: YES ☐ NO ☐

COMMITMENT FOR TOMORROW MORNING:

POCKET #3

5:40 AM
6:00 AM
GROW

COMPLETED: YES ☐ NO ☐

COMMITMENT FOR TOMORROW MORNING:

MORNING PRACTICE

5 MICRO GOALS FOR TODAY:

1.
2.
3.
4.
5.

EVENING PRACTICE

3 TINY WINS OF THIS DAY:

1.
2.
3.

PRE-SLEEP RITUAL DONE: YES ☐ NO ☐

"Problems are just opportunities in wolf's clothing."

-ROBIN SHARMA-

MY DAILY REFLECTION

DAY 87/90

— THE 20/20/20 FORMULA™ —

POCKET #1

5:00 AM
5:20 AM
MOVE

COMPLETED: YES ☐ NO ☐

COMMITMENT FOR TOMORROW MORNING:

POCKET #2

5:20 AM
5:40 AM
REFLECT

COMPLETED: YES ☐ NO ☐

COMMITMENT FOR TOMORROW MORNING:

POCKET #3

5:40 AM
6:00 AM
GROW

COMPLETED: YES ☐ NO ☐

COMMITMENT FOR TOMORROW MORNING:

MORNING PRACTICE

5 MICRO GOALS FOR TODAY:

1.
2.
3.
4.
5.

EVENING PRACTICE

3 TINY WINS OF THIS DAY:

1.
2.
3.

PRE-SLEEP RITUAL DONE: YES ☐ NO ☐

"You have a hero inside of you."
-ROBIN SHARMA-

MY DAILY REFLECTION

DAY 88/90

— THE 20/20/20 FORMULA™ —

POCKET #1

5:00 AM
5:20 AM
MOVE

COMPLETED: YES ☐ NO ☐

COMMITMENT FOR TOMORROW MORNING:

POCKET #2

5:20 AM
5:40 AM
REFLECT

COMPLETED: YES ☐ NO ☐

COMMITMENT FOR TOMORROW MORNING:

POCKET #3

5:40 AM
6:00 AM
GROW

COMPLETED: YES ☐ NO ☐

COMMITMENT FOR TOMORROW MORNING:

MORNING PRACTICE

5 MICRO GOALS FOR TODAY:

1.
2.
3.
4.
5.

EVENING PRACTICE

3 TINY WINS OF THIS DAY:

1.
2.
3.

PRE-SLEEP RITUAL DONE: YES ☐ NO ☐

"Winning without helping is losing."

- ROBIN SHARMA -

MY DAILY REFLECTION

DAY 89/90

— THE 20/20/20 FORMULA™ —

POCKET #1

5:00 AM
5:20 AM
MOVE

COMPLETED: YES ☐ NO ☐

COMMITMENT FOR TOMORROW MORNING:

POCKET #2

5:20 AM
5:40 AM
REFLECT

COMPLETED: YES ☐ NO ☐

COMMITMENT FOR TOMORROW MORNING:

POCKET #3

5:40 AM
6:00 AM
GROW

COMPLETED: YES ☐ NO ☐

COMMITMENT FOR TOMORROW MORNING:

MORNING PRACTICE

5 MICRO GOALS FOR TODAY:

1.
2.
3.
4.
5.

EVENING PRACTICE

3 TINY WINS OF THIS DAY:

1.
2.
3.

PRE-SLEEP RITUAL DONE: YES ☐ NO ☐

"With practice, you can turn down the volume of the voice of your scared self. And increase the tone of your most triumphant side."

-ROBIN SHARMA-

MY DAILY REFLECTION

DAY 90/90

— THE 20/20/20 FORMULA™ —

POCKET #1

5:00 AM
–
5:20 AM
MOVE

COMPLETED: YES ☐ NO ☐

COMMITMENT FOR TOMORROW MORNING:

POCKET #2

5:20 AM
–
5:40 AM
REFLECT

COMPLETED: YES ☐ NO ☐

COMMITMENT FOR TOMORROW MORNING:

POCKET #3

5:40 AM
–
6:00 AM
GROW

COMPLETED: YES ☐ NO ☐

COMMITMENT FOR TOMORROW MORNING:

MORNING PRACTICE

5 MICRO GOALS FOR TODAY:

1.
2.
3.
4.
5.

EVENING PRACTICE

3 TINY WINS OF THIS DAY:

1.
2.
3.

PRE-SLEEP RITUAL DONE: YES ☐ NO ☐

"Each early morning is a page in the story that becomes your legacy."

-ROBIN SHARMA-

MY DAILY REFLECTION

30 DAY PERFORMANCE INQUIRY

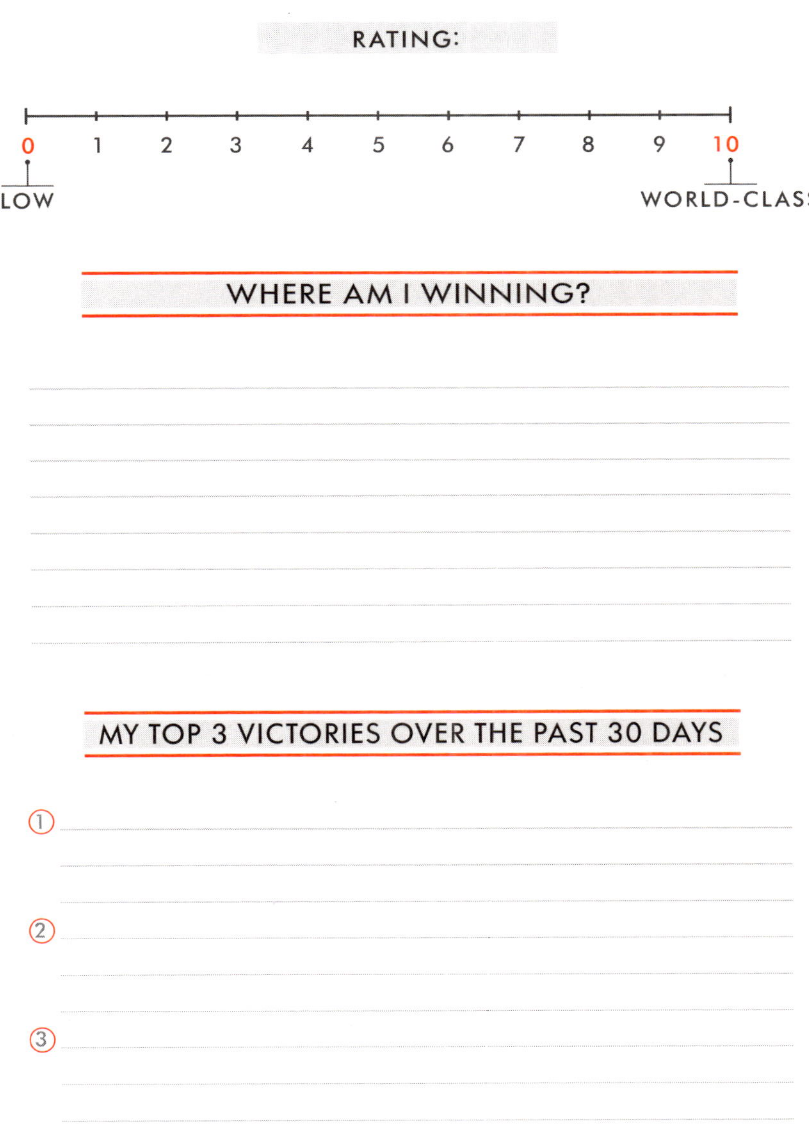

MY IDEAL NEXT 30 DAYS AS A DRAWING

5 PROGRESS ACCELERATORS THAT WILL MAKE THE NEXT 30 DAYS MY BEST 30 DAYS YET

1.

2.

3.

4.

5.

READY TO MAXIMIZE YOUR MORNING MASTERY?

NOTES + IDEAS

OWN YOUR MORNING ELEVATE YOUR LIFE